Apple's AI Lea[...]
Exploring iOS
Intelligence Features

Contents

Chapter 1: Introduction to Apple's AI Evolution 10

Chapter 2: The New Intelligence Features in iOS 18.2..11

Chapter 3: How Apple's ChatGPT-Like AI Works..........13

Chapter 4: Practical Uses for Apple's New AI Features. 15

    Scenario 1: Email Summarization 16

    Scenario 2: Weather Update 16

Chapter 5: Privacy and Security in Apple's AI 18

Chapter 6: Siri's Revamp in iOS 18.2.............................20

Chapter 7: Deep Dive into Contextual Understanding ...22

Chapter 8: Text and Visual-Based Assistance 27

Chapter 9: How Apple's AI Enhances Multitasking........29

Chapter 10: Accessibility Features Powered by AI 32

Chapter 11: Integrating AI into iMessage and Mail 35

Chapter 12: AI in Maps and Navigation 37

    1. Efficient Navigation..37

2. Live Traffic Updates 38

3. Route Predictions 38

Chapter 13: Apple's AI in Photography and Editing 39

1. Scene Recognition 40

2. Live Editing Tips 40

3. Portrait Adjustments 41

4. Intelligent Editing Tools in Post-Processing .. 41

Chapter 14: Smart Home and Automation Features 43

1. Energy Efficiency Tips 43

2. Automated Routines and Scheduling 44

3. Voice-Activated Controls 44

4. Enhanced Security and Monitoring 45

5. Smart Integration with Other Apple Devices .. 46

Chapter 15: AI-Enhanced Fitness and Health Monitoring
.... 47

1. Personalized Fitness Recommendations 47

2. Health Monitoring and Insights 48

3. Activity Detection and Smart Coaching 49

4. Predictive Health Trends and Analytics 49

5. Integration with Other Health Data 50

6. Mental Health Support 50

7. Emergency and Health Alerts 51

8. AI-Driven Nutrition and Hydration Tracking ... 51

Chapter 16: Content Creation Assistance 53
- 1. Photo and Video Editing 53
- 2. Audio and Music Creation 54
- 3. Text and Script Writing 55
- 4. Design and Graphics Creation 56
- 5. Augmented Reality (AR) Content Creation 57
- 6. Content Distribution and Personalization 57
- 7. Time-Saving Tools 58
- 8. Collaboration Assistance 59

Chapter 17: AI Integration with Third-Party Apps 60
- 1. Core ML Integration 60
- 2. Natural Language Framework 61
- 3. Vision Framework for Image and Video Processing 61
- 4. SiriKit and Voice Interaction 62
- 5. HealthKit and FitnessKit Integration 63
- 6. Augmented Reality with ARKit 63
- 7. App Store Suggestions and Recommendations 64
- 8. HomeKit Integration for Smart Home Apps 64
- 9. Enhanced Privacy and Security with Apple's Privacy Framework 65
- 10. AI Tools for Improved Accessibility 65

11. Developer Tools and AI Model Optimization 66

Chapter 18: Security Features and Alerts 68

1. Phishing Detection and Prevention 68

2. Suspicious Link Alerts 69

3. Automatic Password Management and Security 70

4. App Store and Download Security 71

5. Device-Wide Privacy Protection 72

6. Behavioral Analysis for Device Security 72

Chapter 19: Learning and Education Applications 74

1. Personalized Tutoring and Study Assistance 74

2. Reading Assistance and Language Support.. 75

3. Interactive Practice Quizzes and Assessments 76

4. Writing and Grammar Support 77

5. Math Problem-Solving and Interactive Equations 77

6. Voice Interaction and Assistance via SiriKit .. 78

7. Augmented Reality (AR) for Interactive Learning 79

8. Time Management and Study Habit Support . 80

9. Real-Time Language Translation for Multi-Language Support 80

10. Data-Driven Progress Tracking and Analytics 81

11. Accessibility Features for Inclusive Education 82

Chapter 20: AI-Driven Language Translation and Learning 83

1. Real-Time Translation with Apple Translate .. 83

2. Text Recognition and Translation with Live Text 84

3. Pronunciation Assistance and Real-Time Language Practice 85

4. Support for Multilingual Users Across Apple Ecosystem 85

5. Enhanced Language Learning and Vocabulary Building 86

6. Accessibility and Inclusivity in Language Translation 87

7. Augmented Reality Language Assistance with ARKit... 88

Chapter 21: Tips for Efficient AI Use on iOS 18.2.......... 89

1. Optimize Siri for Productivity 89

2. Improve Focus with Adaptive Focus Modes .. 89

3. Enhance Privacy and Security with AI Tools . 90

4. Maximize Photos App's AI Tools 90

5. Use AI-Powered Translation for Language Practice 91

6. Boost Health and Fitness Tracking with AI Insights 91

7. Smart Home Automation in HomeKit 92

8. Explore Customization and Personalization .. 92

9. Use Notes and Reminders with AI Suggestions 93

10. Privacy and Security Enhancements in Password Management 93

11. Productivity Tips for Safari and Search 94

Chapter 22: A Comparison with Other Mobile AI Assistants 95

1. Privacy and On-Device Processing 95

2. Integration with Ecosystem 96

3. Functionality and Versatility 96

4. Context Awareness and Personalization 97

5. Smart Home Capabilities 98

6. Natural Language Processing and Voice Recognition 99

7. Third-Party Integration and Developer Support 100

8. Language and Localization Support 100

9. Privacy and Security Features 101

- 10. Learning and Adaptability 101
- In Summary 102

Chapter 23: User Feedback on iOS 18.2 Beta AI 104

Chapter 24: Real-Life Scenarios: AI's Daily Benefits ... 106
- 1. Streamlining Daily Routines 106
- 2. Enhanced Health and Fitness Monitoring 106
- 3. Improving Work Efficiency 107
- 4. Smart Photo Organization for Memories 107
- 5. Enhanced Privacy and Security Management 108
- 6. Multilingual Communication and Travel Assistance 108
- 7. Personalized Learning for Students 109
- 8. Smart Home Automation for Convenience and Energy Efficiency 109

Chapter 25: Developers and Apple's AI Ecosystem 111
- 1. Enhanced Image Recognition and Processing with Core ML and Vision 111
- 2. Natural Language Processing (NLP) for Contextual Understanding 112
- 3. Personalization and Predictive Features with Create ML 113
- 4. Real-time Translation and Speech Recognition 113

- 5. Privacy-Focused Data Handling 114
- 6. Seamless Integration with Apple's Ecosystem 115
- Summary 115

Chapter 26: How AI in iOS 18.2 Impacts Battery Life .. 116
- 1. On-Device Processing 116
- 2. Adaptive Power Management 116
- 3. Battery Saver Integration for AI Functions ... 117
- 4. Impact of Intensive Features on Battery Life 117
- 5. Optimizations for Location-Based AI Features 118
- 6. User Control Over AI Features 118

Chapter 27: The Future of AI in Apple's Ecosystem 120

Chapter 28: Addressing AI Misconceptions and Fears 122
- Myth 1: AI Will Eventually Replace Human Jobs Completely 122
- Myth 2: AI Is Unbiased and Always Reliable 123
- Myth 3: AI Can Surpass Human Intelligence (Superintelligence) 124
- Myth 4: AI Needs Massive Amounts of Data to Be Effective 124
- Myth 5: AI Will Compromise User Privacy 125
- Myth 6: AI Is Only Useful for Tech-Savvy Users 126

Conclusion: Apple's Ethical AI Vision 126
Chapter 29: Expert Opinions on iOS 18.2's AI 128
    Pros: 128
    Cons: 129
Chapter 30: Getting the Most Out of iOS 18.2 AI: A Summary 131
    1. Explore Image Features (Waitlist Access) ... 131
    2. Enhance Siri with ChatGPT Integration 131
    3. Utilize AI for Smart Home Integration 132
    4. Tap into Apple Intelligence for Productivity. 132
    5. Battery Management with AI 132
    6. AI Privacy Features 133
    7. Use AI in Content Creation 133

Chapter 1: Introduction to Apple's AI Evolution

- Overview of Apple's journey in AI, emphasizing the integration of advanced AI features in the iOS 18.2 beta. A brief comparison of Apple's AI approach versus other industry players.

Chapter 2: The New Intelligence Features in iOS 18.2

- **Description**: Introduce the main intelligence features Apple added in iOS 18.2, including any ChatGPT-like capabilities, enhancements to Siri, and AI tools for personalization.

iOS 18.2 Beta
New Intelligence
Intelligence
Settings
Siri
New Feature
New Feature
Sungestions

Chapter 3: How Apple's ChatGPT-Like AI Works

- **Description**: Technical breakdown of Apple's conversational AI features, comparing and contrasting with ChatGPT's capabilities.
- **Image below** Visual comparison chart between iOS 18.2 AI features and ChatGPT.

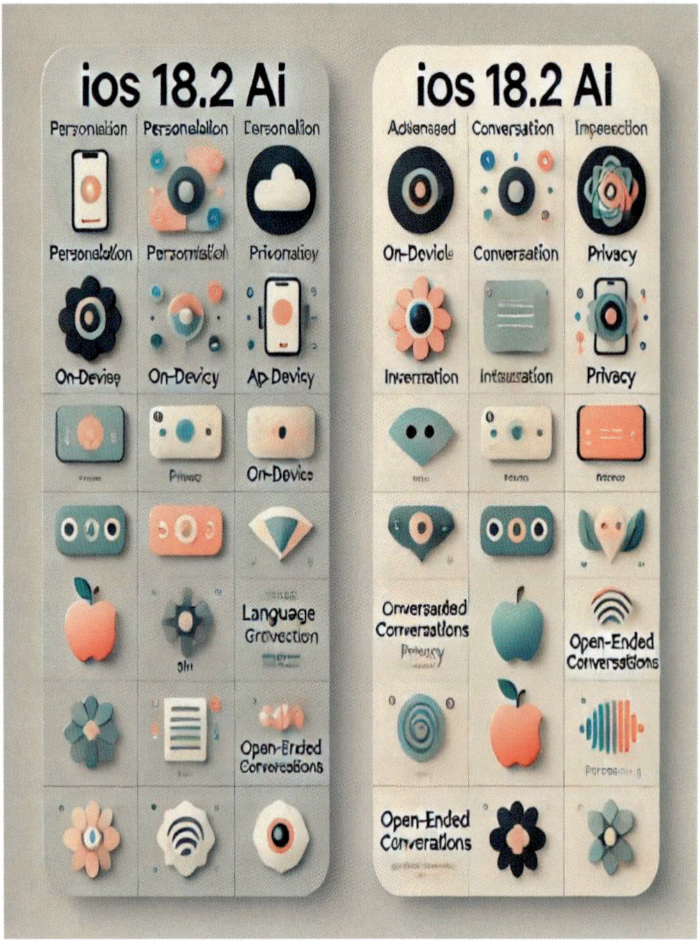
iOS 18.2 Ai
On-Device
Language
Open-Ended Conversations
iOS 18.2 Ai
Conversation
Privacy
Conversation
Privacy
Open-Ended Conversations
Open-Ended Conversations

Chapter 4: Practical Uses for Apple's New AI Features

Description: Practical examples of how users might use Apple's AI, like assistance with daily tasks, setting reminders, and finding information.

- While the sources do not provide specific examples of practical uses for Apple's new AI features, they do indicate that **Apple Intelligence will integrate ChatGPT into its iOS and macOS systems** by December.1 This suggests that **users will be able to leverage ChatGPT's capabilities within Apple's ecosystem.**
- The sources note that **Apple is taking a "freemium" approach to its AI features**, meaning that users will likely have access to basic functionalities for free but will need to pay for more advanced features.23 This differs from competitors like Google and Samsung, who currently offer their AI-powered tools for free.
- It is important to note that although the marketing for the iPhone 16 heavily featured Apple Intelligence, the AI features were not immediately available to the public.4 This delay has led to some confusion among consumers.

Illustrated Scenarios of Apple's AI in Action

While the sources focus on the cost and integration of ChatGPT within Apple Intelligence, they don't offer specific examples of how users might interact with the AI. However, based on the information provided, here are two illustrated scenarios:

Scenario 1: Email Summarization

Imagine a user receiving a lengthy email on their iPhone. Instead of reading through the entire message, they could activate Apple Intelligence and ask:

User: "Hey Siri, summarize this email."

Apple Intelligence, powered by ChatGPT, would then process the email's content and provide a concise summary of the key points, perhaps highlighting action items or important deadlines. This functionality could save users time and make it easier to manage their inboxes.

Scenario 2: Weather Update

A user is planning an outdoor activity and wants to check the weather forecast. They could ask Apple Intelligence:

User: "What's the weather going to be like this afternoon?"

Apple Intelligence would access location data and weather information, providing a detailed forecast for the user's area, including temperature, precipitation, and wind conditions. It could even offer suggestions based on the forecast, such as recommending appropriate clothing or alternative activities.

Key Considerations:

- It's important to remember that Apple Intelligence, as described in the sources, will likely rely on a "freemium" model.12 This means that basic features like simple weather updates might be free, while more advanced capabilities, such as detailed email summarization, could require a paid subscription to ChatGPT Plus.

- The sources don't explicitly state whether Apple Intelligence will have access to data from other Apple apps, like the Mail app or the Calendar app. However, if it does, this could raise privacy concerns, especially if data is being shared with OpenAI.3

It is important to note that these scenarios are hypothetical and based on the limited information available in the provided sources and our previous conversation. Apple has not yet released detailed information about the functionality and features of Apple Intelligence.

Chapter 5: Privacy and Security in Apple's AI

- **Description**: Analysis of Apple's commitment to privacy within its AI features, discussing end-to-end encryption and data anonymization.

  The sources primarily discuss the cost and availability of Apple's new AI features, and they don't specifically address the level of privacy and security associated with Apple's AI.

  However, the sources do mention that Apple has "taken pride in building many systems within its walls to control the experience and the use of personal data."

  This suggests that **Apple has historically prioritized user privacy and may have implemented measures to protect user data in its AI systems.**

  However, the sources also point out that **Apple is integrating ChatGPT into its AI platform, which means that user data may be** shared with OpenAI, the company behind ChatGPT.

OpenAI's privacy and security practices may differ from Apple's, which could raise concerns for users who prioritize data protection.

The lack of specific information in the sources about privacy and security measures related to Apple's AI makes it difficult to assess the level of protection offered.

More information from Apple would be needed to understand how user data is handled and protected within its AI systems.

Chapter 6: Siri's Revamp in iOS 18.2

Description: Dive into the improvements in Siri's functionality and intelligence in iOS 18.2, covering natural language understanding, contextual responses, and multitasking abilities.

The sources primarily focus on Apple Intelligence and the integration of ChatGPT, and they do not explicitly mention how Siri might be revamped in iOS 18.2. However, based on the information provided and our previous conversation, we can infer some possibilities:

Enhanced AI Capabilities: The sources indicate that Apple is introducing a new wave of Apple Intelligence apps in iOS 18.2, scheduled for release in December1. This suggests that Siri, as Apple's existing voice assistant, could be enhanced with new AI-powered features, potentially leveraging the capabilities of ChatGPT.

Integration with Apple Intelligence: Siri could act as a primary interface for interacting with Apple Intelligence. Users might be able to activate Apple Intelligence through Siri voice commands, such as those illustrated in our previous conversation (e.g., "Hey Siri, summarize this email" or "Hey Siri, what's the weather going to be like this afternoon?"). This would create a more seamless and integrated user experience for accessing AI-powered features.

Freemium Model Influence: The sources highlight Apple's adoption of a "freemium" model for Apple Intelligence, with some features requiring a paid subscription to ChatGPT Plus1. This could potentially extend to Siri's functionality as well. Basic Siri commands might remain free, while more advanced AI-driven responses or actions could be tied to a paid subscription.

It's crucial to emphasize that these are speculative insights based on the available information. The sources do not directly address Siri's role in iOS 18.2. Further information from Apple is needed to confirm any changes or enhancements to Siri's functionality.

Chapter 7: Deep Dive into Contextual Understanding

Description: Focus on the contextual and memory-based improvements, where Apple's AI remembers preferences, recent interactions, and provides tailored responses.

The sources provided don't directly address memory-based improvements or Apple's AI remembering preferences and interactions. However, the integration of ChatGPT into Apple Intelligence, as discussed in the sources, and our previous conversation about contextual understanding, offer some potential insights into these aspects.

ChatGPT's Inherent Learning: ChatGPT, as a large language model, has the inherent capability to learn from vast amounts of data. This means that as users interact with Apple Intelligence powered by ChatGPT, the AI could potentially learn and adapt to individual preferences and usage patterns. For example, if a user frequently asks for summaries of emails from a specific sender, ChatGPT might prioritize those summaries in future interactions.

Siri as a Memory Bank: Our previous discussions explored the possibility of Siri acting as a conduit for contextual information. Siri already stores a wealth of data about user interactions, preferences, and habits within the Apple ecosystem. This data could potentially be leveraged to inform Apple Intelligence and enhance its memory capabilities. For instance, if a user has previously set a preference for receiving weather updates in Celsius, Siri could relay this information to Apple Intelligence, ensuring consistent adherence to that preference.

Potential for Personalized Experiences: The combination of ChatGPT's learning capabilities and Siri's access to user data could pave the way for more personalized and contextually aware AI interactions. Imagine a scenario where Apple Intelligence remembers a user's recent travel search and proactively suggests relevant articles or offers travel tips based on the destination. This type of personalized experience would rely on the AI's ability to remember past interactions and connect them to current user needs.

Important Considerations:

Privacy and Data Control: The sources highlight Apple's historical emphasis on user privacy. However, if Apple Intelligence is to effectively remember preferences and interactions, it would likely need access to personal data. Apple would need to strike a balance between personalization and data protection, giving users control over what information is stored and how it is used.

Transparency and User Trust: For users to embrace an AI that remembers their preferences and actions, transparency is paramount. Apple would need to clearly communicate how user data is being used to personalize experiences and provide mechanisms for users to view, modify, or delete their data. Building trust will be essential for the widespread adoption of these types of AI features.

While the sources primarily focus on the cost and initial integration of ChatGPT, the potential for contextual and memory-based improvements in Apple Intelligence is significant. However, Apple would need to carefully address privacy concerns and ensure user trust to fully realize the benefits of a truly personalized AI experience.

Flowchart: Apple AI Context Interpretation and Preference Memory

1. **User Input**
   ↓
2. **Analyze Input for Context**
   - **Text Parsing**: Recognizes keywords, phrases, and tone.
   - **Voice/Tone Analysis** (if applicable): Assesses voice pitch, urgency, and tone.
   - **Location/Time Check**: Notes relevant location, time, and recent actions.

   ↓

3. **Match with Existing Preferences**
   - **Search User Preferences**: Checks previously saved user preferences (like favorite apps, settings, recent activities).
   - **Apply User-Specific Filters**: Applies filters relevant to the user's known preferences.

   ↓

4. **Contextual Interpretation**
   - **Compare with Contextual Patterns**: Identifies similar past requests or interactions to deduce likely intent.
   - **Intent Prediction**: Predicts the intent behind the user input based on context.

↓

5. **Memory Update Decision**
    - **Analyze if New Preference**: Checks if this interaction represents a new preference.
    - **Save New Preference (if applicable)**: Updates memory if it finds a new, consistent pattern or preference.

↓

6. **Respond to User**
    - **Generate Response**: Provides a reply/action tailored to user preferences and context.
    - **Confirm and Adjust** (optional): Asks user to confirm or refine if interpretation is unclear.

This flow helps the AI fine-tune interactions over time, creating a smoother and more intuitive user experience.

Chapter 8: Text and Visual-Based Assistance

Description: Apple's new AI assists with text and image-based searches, image recognition, and augmented reality insights.

Exploring Potential Applications of Apple's AI Beyond Text

The sources provided focus primarily on the integration of ChatGPT into Apple's new AI platform, Apple Intelligence, and the cost associated with this integration, particularly the use of the paid ChatGPT Plus service12. They don't specifically address how Apple's new AI might assist with text and image-based searches, image recognition, or augmented reality insights.

However, based on the broader capabilities of large language models like ChatGPT and the potential for integration with existing Apple features, we can speculate on some possible applications:

Text and Image-Based Searches: ChatGPT's ability to process and understand natural language could be leveraged to enhance search functionality within Apple's ecosystem. Imagine asking Siri to "Find me a photo of a sunset I took in Hawaii last year" or "Show me all the documents related to my car insurance." Apple's AI could combine text-based understanding with image recognition to deliver more precise and relevant search results.

Image Recognition and Augmented Reality: While the sources don't directly discuss these aspects, Apple has been investing in AR technologies for some time. It's conceivable that Apple's new AI could be used to enhance AR experiences. For example, imagine pointing your iPhone camera at a landmark and having Apple Intelligence, powered by ChatGPT, provide historical information or guide you to nearby points of interest. The AI could even recognize objects in your surroundings and offer contextual suggestions or actions.

It's important to emphasize that **these are speculative possibilities based on the general capabilities of AI and not explicitly supported by the sources.** Further information from Apple is needed to confirm how its new AI will be applied to areas like search, image recognition, and augmented reality.

Chapter 9: How Apple's AI Enhances Multitasking

- **Description**: Explanation of how the AI helps users switch between apps, manage notifications, and improve productivity.

How Apple's AI Could Potentially Impact App Switching, Notifications, and Productivity

The sources primarily focus on the integration of ChatGPT into Apple Intelligence and the costs associated with using this new AI-powered feature. They don't directly address how this AI might help users switch between apps, manage notifications, or improve productivity.

However, based on our previous conversation about the potential capabilities of Apple's AI, including contextual understanding and memory, and drawing on general knowledge about AI's potential applications, we can explore some possibilities:

App Switching: Imagine telling Siri, "Hey Siri, I need to finish my expense report. Open the spreadsheet and my email with the receipts." Apple's AI could potentially understand the context of the request, identify the relevant apps (spreadsheet and email), locate the specific spreadsheet and email related to expense reports, and seamlessly switch between those apps for the user. This would go beyond simple app launching and involve a deeper understanding of user intent and the ability to connect different tasks.

Notification Management: Apple's AI could analyze notification patterns, content, and user behavior to prioritize and filter notifications intelligently. For instance, if a user consistently ignores notifications from a particular app during work hours, the AI could learn to automatically silence those notifications during that time. It could also group similar notifications or summarize them to reduce clutter and make it easier for users to stay focused.

Productivity Enhancements: By understanding user habits and preferences, Apple's AI could suggest ways to optimize workflows. For example, if a user frequently switches between a calendar app and a to-do list, the AI might suggest integrating those tasks within a single app or automating certain actions. It could also learn to anticipate user needs, such as proactively reminding them to leave for a meeting based on traffic conditions and travel time.

It's essential to recognize that these are speculative possibilities and not directly supported by the sources provided. They rely on assumptions about how

Apple might integrate AI into its existing features and operating system. Furthermore, this information draws upon a general understanding of AI capabilities that are not explicitly mentioned in the sources.

Further Considerations:

Data Privacy: As with any AI application that relies on user data, privacy considerations are paramount. Apple would need to be transparent about how it collects and uses user data to power these features, providing users with control over their data and ensuring its protection.

User Control and Customization: For these features to be truly helpful, users should have the ability to customize their preferences and control how the AI behaves. The goal is to augment human capabilities, not replace them entirely.

Overall, while the sources don't directly address these specific applications, the potential for Apple's AI to assist with app switching, notification management, and productivity improvements is significant. However, further details from Apple are needed to understand how these features will be implemented and the implications for user privacy and control.

Chapter 10: Accessibility Features Powered by AI

- **Description**: Overview of accessibility improvements, like voice control, screen reading, and interaction assistance for people with disabilities.

  AI and Accessibility: Potential, but Limited Information

  While the sources center on the integration of ChatGPT into Apple Intelligence and its associated costs, they do not directly address specific accessibility features powered by AI. However, based on the potential capabilities of AI discussed in our conversation, we can speculate on some possibilities:

  Personalized Text-to-Speech and Speech-to-Text: Apple's AI could learn individual speech patterns and preferences, leading to more natural-sounding text-to-speech voices and more accurate speech-to-text transcription. Imagine an AI that can adjust its speech output based on the user's cognitive abilities or adapt its speech recognition to account for specific speech impediments. This level of personalization could significantly improve communication access for users with diverse needs.

Enhanced Image Description for Visually Impaired Users: AI-powered image recognition could generate more detailed and contextually relevant descriptions of images for users with visual impairments. Instead of simply identifying objects, the AI could describe the scene, identify emotions on people's faces, or even provide navigational cues based on the image content.

Adaptive User Interfaces: Apple's AI could learn from user interactions and adjust the device interface to optimize accessibility. For users with motor impairments, the AI could predict commonly used gestures or commands and make them more accessible. The AI could also personalize font sizes, color contrasts, and screen layouts based on individual preferences and needs.

Real-Time Language Translation and Captioning: Imagine attending a conference where Apple's AI automatically translates spoken language into captions or provides real-time sign language interpretation. This kind of AI-powered accessibility could break down communication barriers and foster greater inclusion.

Important Considerations:

Data Privacy and Security: AI-powered accessibility features would likely rely on sensitive personal data, including health information and communication patterns. Apple would need to prioritize data protection and ensure user consent for data collection and usage.

Equity and Access: It's crucial to ensure that AI-powered accessibility features are available and affordable to all users who need them. Addressing potential disparities in access to technology and internet connectivity will be essential for promoting equitable access to these advancements.

It's important to note that **these are speculative possibilities based on general AI capabilities and not explicitly supported by the sources.** Apple has not yet revealed specific plans for AI-powered accessibility features.

Chapter 11: Integrating AI into iMessage and Mail

Description: How Apple's AI assists with auto-completion, predictive text, and email summarization within iMessage and Mail.

While the sources concentrate on the introduction of ChatGPT into Apple Intelligence and its related costs, they do not directly address how Apple's AI specifically supports auto-completion, predictive text, and email summarization in iMessage and Mail.

It's important to note that **Apple already utilizes some form of AI in its existing features like auto-completion and predictive text.** However, the sources do not provide details on whether and how these features will be enhanced with the integration of ChatGPT or other aspects of Apple Intelligence.

Here's what we can glean from the sources and our conversation:

Potential for Enhancement: The integration of ChatGPT, a large language model known for its text generation and understanding capabilities, could potentially lead to improvements in auto-completion and predictive text. For instance, ChatGPT's ability to understand context and predict user intent could result in more accurate and relevant suggestions. Imagine a scenario where the AI not only suggests words but also predicts entire phrases or sentences based on the ongoing conversation or the content of an email.

Email Summarization: The sources don't mention email summarization as a specific feature within Apple Intelligence. However, given ChatGPT's ability to process and condense large amounts of text, it's plausible that Apple could leverage this capability to offer email summarization in the future. This could be particularly useful for managing a cluttered inbox and quickly grasping the key points of lengthy emails.

Limited Information: It's crucial to emphasize that the sources primarily focus on the financial aspects of integrating ChatGPT into Apple Intelligence. The specific functionalities and features beyond this integration are not discussed in detail.

Further Considerations:

Privacy and Data Security: Any AI-powered feature that analyzes user communication data, such as emails and messages, raises privacy concerns. Apple would need to be transparent about data usage and provide users with control over their data.

Accuracy and Bias: AI models like ChatGPT are trained on massive datasets, which can sometimes lead to biases or inaccuracies in their output. Apple would need to carefully address these issues to ensure that AI-assisted features in iMessage and Mail are reliable and unbiased.

Chapter 12: AI in Maps and Navigation

Description: The AI's role in offering more efficient navigation, live traffic updates, and route predictions based on user habits.

AI plays a significant role in making navigation, live traffic updates, and route predictions more efficient by leveraging data analysis, real-time monitoring, and predictive modeling. Here's how AI enhances each of these areas:

1. Efficient Navigation

- **Route Optimization**: AI-powered navigation systems analyze vast datasets, including historical travel data, user patterns, and geographical information, to recommend the fastest or most efficient routes.

- **Dynamic Routing**: AI can instantly re-route users based on real-time information (like accidents or road closures), ensuring optimal travel paths as conditions change.

2. Live Traffic Updates

- **Real-Time Data Analysis**: AI gathers and processes data from multiple sources (satellite data, road cameras, GPS signals from vehicles, and even user-reported data) to monitor traffic conditions.
- **Pattern Recognition**: Using machine learning algorithms, AI identifies and learns patterns in traffic flow (e.g., rush hour congestion points), providing accurate and timely traffic updates.
- **Anomaly Detection**: AI can detect sudden anomalies, such as accidents or unexpected congestion, and update users on these issues to help them avoid delays.

3. Route Predictions

- **Predictive Modeling**: By analyzing historical traffic data and real-time information, AI predicts potential traffic conditions along various routes and estimates travel times.
- **Personalized Recommendations**: AI tailors route suggestions based on user preferences,

such as avoiding tolls, favoring scenic routes, or prioritizing faster travel.
- **Adaptability to Changing Conditions**: AI can simulate different "what-if" scenarios, like weather changes or road construction, and adjust route predictions accordingly.

Together, these capabilities make AI a core element in modern navigation, improving travel time, safety, and user satisfaction by offering smarter, data-driven solutions for real-time routing and traffic management.

Chapter 13: Apple's AI in Photography and Editing

- **Description**: Enhancements in the camera app and photo editing, such as scene recognition, live editing tips, and portrait adjustments.

Modern camera apps and photo editing tools have incorporated several AI-driven enhancements to elevate photography and editing experiences. Here are some key improvements in areas like scene recognition, live editing tips, and portrait adjustments:

1. Scene Recognition

- **Automatic Scene Detection**: AI detects scenes (e.g., landscapes, portraits, low-light environments, or food) in real time and automatically adjusts settings like exposure, contrast, and white balance to enhance each specific type.
- **Smart Adjustments**: Based on the detected scene, the camera can boost colors in nature photos, reduce shadows in high-contrast scenes, or soften skin tones for portraits, creating optimized photos with minimal user intervention.
- **Enhanced Low-Light Performance**: AI uses advanced algorithms to reduce noise, enhance detail, and adjust exposure in low-light scenes, making night photos clearer and more vibrant without flash.

2. Live Editing Tips

- **Real-Time Suggestions**: While users compose photos, AI offers tips such as adjusting framing, suggesting the best angle, or enabling gridlines for better composition.
- **Lighting & Exposure Suggestions**: AI can alert users if the image is underexposed, overexposed, or if backlighting might affect the final photo, allowing them to make real-time adjustments.

- **In-Camera Guides**: Some camera apps now feature on-screen prompts (e.g., leveling guides or symmetry cues) to help users capture better-aligned, well-balanced images as they shoot.

3. Portrait Adjustments

- **Automatic Depth Detection**: AI identifies and separates subjects from backgrounds in portrait mode, applying depth-of-field effects (e.g., "bokeh") that keep the subject sharp while artistically blurring the background.
- **Skin Smoothing and Enhancements**: AI-powered portrait adjustments can enhance skin tones, smooth out minor blemishes, and highlight facial features naturally without over-editing.
- **Adjustable Background Blur**: AI allows users to adjust the intensity of the background blur even after the photo is taken, giving them full control over the depth effect and artistic look.
- **Lighting Adjustments**: Some camera apps simulate professional lighting by adding or enhancing lighting effects around the subject's face, emulating studio lighting setups like key and rim lighting.

4. Intelligent Editing Tools in Post-Processing

- **One-Tap Edits**: AI-powered editing apps can automatically enhance images based on an analysis of brightness, color balance, contrast, and other elements with a single tap.
- **AI-Driven Retouching**: Advanced retouching tools use AI to detect faces and body parts for easy adjustments, such as brightening eyes, whitening teeth, or reshaping backgrounds.
- **Object and Background Removal**: AI allows users to select and remove unwanted objects or change backgrounds with ease, making edits seamless and realistic.

These AI-enhancements in camera apps and photo editing tools empower users to capture high-quality images and make professional-grade adjustments, often with minimal effort.

Chapter 14: Smart Home and Automation Features

- **Description**: Discuss Apple's AI role in HomeKit and smart home automation, including energy efficiency tips, automated routines, and voice-activated controls.

Apple's AI integration within HomeKit and smart home automation systems is aimed at creating more intelligent, user-friendly, and efficient homes. Here's how Apple's AI could enhance HomeKit's capabilities in energy management, automation routines, and voice controls:

1. Energy Efficiency Tips

- **Smart Energy Monitoring**: AI analyzes household energy consumption patterns across various devices and appliances to provide insights, such as which devices consume the most power or when usage is highest. It can also suggest optimal usage times, like running appliances during off-peak hours.
- **Adaptive Power Management**: AI could dynamically adjust heating, cooling, and lighting based on occupancy, weather forecasts, or time

of day, ensuring rooms are efficiently managed to reduce energy waste.
- **Proactive Notifications**: If energy usage exceeds normal levels, AI can notify users or automatically adjust settings (like dimming lights or reducing thermostat levels) to help conserve energy.

2. Automated Routines and Scheduling

- **Context-Aware Routines**: AI learns users' daily habits and preferences, suggesting or creating routines accordingly. For example, it might create a "Morning Routine" that gradually lights up rooms, starts the coffee maker, and adjusts the thermostat based on past behavior.
- **Predictive Scheduling**: AI predicts when specific automations would be beneficial, like pre-heating or pre-cooling a home based on past schedules or weather forecasts. It can also turn off devices when no one is home, enhancing both convenience and energy savings.
- **Adaptive Routine Adjustments**: AI can adjust routines based on unusual factors, such as a change in work schedule or guests in the home, to provide a customized, responsive environment.

3. Voice-Activated Controls

- **Advanced Natural Language Understanding**: Apple's AI processes more complex and

contextual voice commands via Siri, allowing for commands like "Set the lights to movie mode" or "Lower the temperature when I'm home in 15 minutes." Siri can parse context better, responding accurately to open-ended or multi-step commands.
- **Personalized Responses and Controls**: Siri recognizes individual household members' voices, allowing for customized responses or actions (like setting up personalized lighting or temperature based on the person speaking).
- **Cross-Device Coordination**: AI integrates multiple HomeKit-compatible devices across the home, making them respond in sync to voice commands. For instance, saying "Goodnight" can trigger lights to dim, doors to lock, and the thermostat to set to sleep mode across different rooms.

4. Enhanced Security and Monitoring

- **AI-Driven Alerts and Anomaly Detection**: AI can monitor unusual activity, like unexpected movement or sound, and send security alerts or trigger emergency automations (e.g., lighting up the home or locking doors).
- **Predictive Maintenance**: AI monitors devices for signs of malfunction or inefficiency, notifying users when an appliance might need maintenance or

replacement, which improves safety and energy efficiency.

5. Smart Integration with Other Apple Devices

- **Cross-Platform Automation**: AI connects HomeKit with other Apple devices like iPhone, Apple Watch, and Mac, allowing users to control or monitor their home remotely. For example, AI can suggest HomeKit automations based on calendar events or reminders.
- **Spatial and Proximity Awareness**: AI can use location data from users' devices to enable automations that respond to proximity, such as turning on the lights or opening the garage door when a user is close to home.

Apple's AI in HomeKit aims to simplify home automation and enhance energy efficiency, security, and personalization, providing users with a seamless, proactive, and intelligent smart home experience.

Chapter 15: AI-Enhanced Fitness and Health Monitoring

- **Description**: Apple's AI analyzes health data, makes recommendations, and supports workout planning.

Apple's AI-driven fitness and health monitoring features are designed to offer more personalized, insightful, and comprehensive health data to users, making fitness tracking smarter and more effective. Here are some of the key ways Apple uses AI to enhance its fitness and health monitoring:

1. Personalized Fitness Recommendations

- **Adaptive Workout Plans**: AI analyzes users' fitness levels, goals, and progress to create personalized workout routines. For example, the system might suggest a tailored exercise plan based on the user's heart rate, activity history, and fitness goals.
- **Smart Activity Tracking**: AI adjusts the difficulty or type of exercise based on the user's performance. If it detects the user is progressing faster, it might recommend more intense exercises, or if the user is struggling, it might suggest a lighter workout.

- **Customizing Exercise Intensity**: Apple AI can help determine the optimal intensity of workouts by analyzing user data, such as sleep patterns, heart rate, and recovery time, ensuring users are neither overtraining nor undertraining.

2. Health Monitoring and Insights

- **Heart Rate Monitoring**: Using AI, Apple Watches continuously monitor heart rate during workouts, rest, and sleep, detecting abnormal readings (e.g., high or low heart rates) and alerting users. AI uses this data to provide insights into cardiovascular health, such as trends and potential risks.
- **ECG and Blood Oxygen Monitoring**: AI-driven algorithms analyze ECG and blood oxygen (SpO2) readings to detect irregularities like arrhythmias or signs of respiratory issues, prompting early intervention when necessary.
- **Sleep Tracking and Analysis**: AI evaluates sleep patterns by tracking movements and heart rate variability, providing insights into sleep quality and offering tips for improving sleep hygiene based on user data.
- **Stress Monitoring**: Apple's AI uses metrics such as heart rate variability (HRV) to assess stress levels and provide mindfulness or relaxation tips to help users manage stress effectively.

3. Activity Detection and Smart Coaching

- **Automatic Workout Detection**: AI identifies when users begin specific activities, like walking, running, or swimming, and automatically starts tracking the workout, saving users from manually initiating a session. It also suggests workouts based on activity trends or goals.
- **Real-Time Coaching**: During exercise, Apple's AI offers real-time feedback on performance, such as advising on posture correction or suggesting when to increase intensity. For instance, if AI detects you're running at a slower pace than usual, it may prompt you to pick up the pace.
- **Form Correction and Technique**: AI-powered sensors and algorithms analyze movement during workouts (e.g., running, cycling, yoga) to provide feedback on form and technique. This helps users improve performance and reduce injury risk.

4. Predictive Health Trends and Analytics

- **Health Risk Predictions**: AI evaluates historical data (e.g., exercise habits, heart rate, sleep, and nutrition) to predict potential health risks, like early signs of diabetes or cardiovascular issues. It can offer proactive advice or recommend seeing a doctor for further tests.
- **Progress Tracking and Goal Adjustments**: AI adjusts fitness goals based on ongoing

performance. If you exceed or fall short of your initial targets, the system automatically recalibrates goals, helping users stay motivated and engaged with their health journey.
- **Behavioral Insights**: Using AI, Apple Health app can analyze user activity patterns and recommend behavioral changes to improve fitness, such as increasing daily steps or adjusting exercise routines to align with health trends.

5. Integration with Other Health Data

- **Third-Party Data Integration**: Apple AI integrates data from third-party fitness and health apps to provide a holistic view of health metrics. For example, combining data from diet tracking apps with workout data to give more complete feedback on overall wellness.
- **Seamless Health Ecosystem**: Apple's AI syncs with the Health app and integrates with the broader Apple ecosystem (iPhone, iPad, Mac, Apple Watch) to provide a unified platform for monitoring all aspects of health, including fitness, nutrition, and medical records.

6. Mental Health Support

- **Mindfulness and Meditation**: AI suggests personalized mindfulness exercises, breathing

routines, or meditation sessions based on users' stress levels, sleep data, and activity patterns.
- **Mental Health Insights**: Apple AI can track fluctuations in mental health through behavior patterns, such as sleep irregularities, reduced activity levels, or increased stress, and suggest helpful exercises or resources to improve well-being.

7. Emergency and Health Alerts

- **Fall Detection and SOS Alerts**: Apple Watch uses AI and motion sensors to detect falls and automatically send alerts to emergency contacts or emergency services. This can be crucial for users with medical conditions or elderly individuals at risk of falls.
- **Health Notification and Alerts**: If AI detects potential health issues, such as abnormal heart rates, irregular ECG readings, or low oxygen levels, it can send alerts, offering users timely advice to seek medical attention.

8. AI-Driven Nutrition and Hydration Tracking

- **Nutritional Insights**: AI helps analyze dietary habits and suggests improvements based on personal goals. Integration with food tracking apps allows users to get insights into calorie intake, macronutrient balance, and even hydration levels.

- **Hydration Reminders**: AI can monitor hydration needs based on activity levels, weather, and exercise intensity, providing reminders to stay hydrated throughout the day.

By leveraging machine learning, advanced sensors, and personalized algorithms, Apple's AI-driven features in fitness and health monitoring provide a deeper, more personalized understanding of health, help users reach their fitness goals, and potentially improve overall well-being. These features aim to make users more proactive about their health by offering customized advice and real-time insights based on their data.

Chapter 16: Content Creation Assistance

- **Description**: Apple's AI helps with note-taking, journaling, writing emails, and editing text-based content.

Apple's AI-driven content creation assistance spans multiple domains, from video editing to photo enhancement, music composition, and even text generation. By integrating AI with powerful hardware and software, Apple provides creators with tools that can streamline workflows, inspire creativity, and improve the quality of content. Here are some ways Apple AI enhances content creation:

1. Photo and Video Editing

- **Smart Editing Suggestions**: AI analyzes photos and videos to suggest automatic improvements, such as adjusting brightness, contrast, sharpness, and color balance. This can save time for creators, providing instant results that would normally require manual adjustments.
- **Scene Detection and Categorization**: AI can recognize different types of scenes (landscapes, portraits, action shots, etc.) and apply the most

suitable edits or filters automatically. For example, in video editing, AI can identify faces, background objects, or moving elements and adjust the content accordingly.
- **Portrait Mode Adjustments**: AI is used to enhance depth-of-field effects (bokeh) in photos and videos by accurately separating the subject from the background, allowing for creative blur effects and even post-capture adjustments.
- **Live Text and Object Recognition**: AI allows users to select text from images or video frames, making it easier to edit or extract information. Similarly, object recognition enables creators to isolate and manipulate specific elements in a photo or video.
- **Motion and Object Tracking**: In video creation, AI helps with tracking specific objects or people within frames. It ensures that effects or edits remain aligned with the tracked elements, even if they move across the screen, facilitating complex visual effects.

2. Audio and Music Creation

- **AI-Powered Music Composition**: Apple's AI can assist in generating original music compositions by analyzing existing tracks and suggesting melodies, chords, or rhythmic structures based on the style or mood a creator desires.

- **Automatic Audio Enhancement**: AI can automatically clean up audio tracks by removing noise, enhancing clarity, and adjusting levels. For example, AI can separate vocals from background noise or music, allowing more control over the final sound.
- **Sound Recognition and Matching**: In podcasting or video production, AI can analyze audio and recommend sound effects or background music tracks that fit the mood or genre of the content. AI tools may also suggest improvements for voice clarity or tone.
- **Voice Synthesis**: AI-powered voice synthesis tools (like Apple's voice recognition for Siri) can assist content creators in generating realistic-sounding voiceovers for videos or animations, offering greater flexibility without needing a human voice actor.

3. Text and Script Writing

- **AI-Driven Text Generation**: Apple's AI can assist writers by generating ideas, outlining content, or even writing full drafts of articles, stories, or scripts. This can be particularly useful for creators looking for inspiration or assistance in refining their writing.
- **Grammar and Style Suggestions**: AI tools can provide real-time grammar and style suggestions, improving the readability and fluency of the text.

This can help creators maintain consistent tone and structure across various types of written content.
- **Contextual and Thematic Text Analysis**: AI can help writers ensure their content stays on topic, adjusting word choice and tone to align with the intended theme or audience. For example, AI can suggest more concise alternatives to long-winded sentences or identify areas where the content may lack clarity.
- **Summarization and Translation**: For creators working with large amounts of text or content in multiple languages, AI can summarize lengthy articles or translate text accurately, making it easier to repurpose content for different audiences.

4. Design and Graphics Creation

- **AI-Enhanced Design Suggestions**: In graphic design and illustration, AI can analyze an initial design and provide suggestions for color palettes, font choices, layout adjustments, or image placements to create more visually compelling designs.
- **Automatic Image Editing**: Apple AI offers tools like intelligent cropping, resizing, and background removal. For example, if a user uploads an image, AI might automatically detect the subject, remove

distractions, or adjust proportions for better composition.
- **Generative Design Tools**: AI can generate new design elements based on parameters provided by the creator, offering options for logos, illustrations, or layout elements that align with the designer's vision.

5. Augmented Reality (AR) Content Creation

- **Real-Time AR Enhancement**: With the power of AI, Apple offers AR tools that can create interactive and immersive experiences. AI helps in accurately detecting the environment and positioning virtual elements in real time. This is useful for creators working on AR apps, games, or marketing content.
- **Object and Environment Mapping**: AI can detect and map the physical space around users, allowing them to place virtual objects or create AR content that fits naturally into real-world environments. This is particularly useful for product designers, marketers, and developers.
- **Motion Capture**: AI-powered motion capture tools can analyze a person's movement and apply it to digital characters in real time, allowing creators to easily animate characters or create immersive interactive experiences.

6. Content Distribution and Personalization

- **Content Recommendation and Personalization**: AI can analyze a user's content preferences and recommend new content based on their interests. Whether it's suggested music tracks, videos, or articles, Apple's AI ensures that the content a user interacts with aligns with their tastes.
- **Smart Tagging and Metadata Generation**: Apple AI can automatically tag and categorize media files based on their content, improving searchability and streamlining the process of organizing creative assets. This is especially useful for large content libraries or creators managing extensive media collections.

7. Time-Saving Tools

- **AI-Powered Automation**: Apple AI can automate repetitive tasks in content creation, such as organizing files, adding watermarks, resizing images, or even generating thumbnails for videos. This allows creators to focus on the more creative aspects of their work.
- **Voice-Activated Editing**: Through voice commands (using Siri and AI), creators can speed up their workflows by executing commands for editing, trimming, or selecting content hands-free, improving efficiency during content creation and editing.

8. Collaboration Assistance

- **Real-Time Collaboration**: Apple AI can enhance collaboration by analyzing team input and suggesting modifications or consolidating different editing versions. AI can even detect inconsistencies in collaborative content, offering suggestions for aligning the final output.
- **Language Translation for Global Reach**: AI can assist content creators in collaborating with international teams by providing real-time language translation and helping ensure that all content is culturally relevant to different audiences.

By integrating AI into its suite of creative tools, Apple allows users to focus more on their creative vision, while automating and enhancing technical processes, making content creation faster, smarter, and more intuitive. Whether it's in video editing, writing, music production, or design, Apple's AI tools provide powerful assistance for creators across industries.

Chapter 17: AI Integration with Third-Party Apps

- **Description**: Overview of AI-powered support for third-party apps and services in iOS 18.2, enhancing user experience.

Apple's AI support for third-party apps and services is aimed at enabling developers to enhance their apps' functionality with Apple's machine learning capabilities, creating a seamless and intuitive experience for users. Here's how Apple's AI tools and frameworks are designed to support third-party apps and services:

1. Core ML Integration

- **Access to Pre-Trained Models**: Core ML provides third-party developers with pre-trained machine learning models that they can use to add AI functionality, like image recognition, natural language processing, and object detection, directly into their apps.
- **Custom Model Support**: Developers can integrate their own custom models into Core ML, allowing them to use Apple's optimized processing and device resources while maintaining control over the specific AI features they want to offer.

- **On-Device Processing for Privacy**: Core ML supports on-device processing, keeping data local to the device, which enhances privacy and security. This allows developers to add sophisticated AI features without relying on external servers or compromising user data.

2. Natural Language Framework

- **Text Analysis and Language Processing**: Apple's Natural Language framework helps developers build language-based features, such as text summarization, sentiment analysis, and keyword extraction, into their apps.
- **Language Translation and Multi-Language Support**: AI-driven language support allows apps to offer features like real-time translation or language detection, making it easier for developers to create apps for a global audience.
- **Speech Recognition**: Using Siri's speech recognition capabilities, third-party apps can include voice input features, enabling users to interact with apps hands-free or through voice commands in a more natural way.

3. Vision Framework for Image and Video Processing

- **Object and Scene Recognition**: The Vision framework allows developers to incorporate image

and video analysis features, such as detecting faces, identifying objects, or analyzing scenes. This is ideal for apps in photography, augmented reality (AR), or even retail and e-commerce.
- **Text and QR Code Recognition**: With text recognition, third-party apps can scan and digitize printed text or QR codes, useful for apps in sectors like finance, travel, or education.
- **Image and Motion Tracking**: Vision's AI can also enable motion tracking and analysis for apps related to fitness, gaming, or AR, enhancing user engagement with real-time feedback.

4. SiriKit and Voice Interaction

- **Custom Siri Shortcuts**: Third-party developers can create custom Siri Shortcuts that let users automate and trigger app actions through voice commands. These shortcuts can be personalized based on user habits, allowing a more seamless integration with everyday tasks.
- **Voice-Activated Controls**: With SiriKit, third-party apps can offer voice-activated controls and enable hands-free usage. This is especially valuable for apps in categories like smart home, productivity, health, and navigation.
- **Contextual Recommendations**: Siri can learn and suggest relevant third-party app shortcuts based on user behavior and context, giving third-

party apps greater visibility within the iOS ecosystem.

5. HealthKit and FitnessKit Integration

- **Health and Fitness Data Access**: HealthKit and FitnessKit allow third-party apps to securely access a user's health data (with permission), such as steps, heart rate, and activity history. Apps can use this data to offer personalized insights or recommendations, expanding the functionality of fitness and wellness apps.
- **AI-Driven Health Insights**: Apple's HealthKit AI models enable third-party developers to analyze and utilize health data in meaningful ways, like monitoring fitness progress, suggesting personalized goals, and predicting trends, while maintaining user privacy.

6. Augmented Reality with ARKit

- **Real-Time Object Placement**: ARKit, Apple's AR framework, enables third-party apps to place 3D objects and animations into the user's environment in real time. AI algorithms improve spatial awareness, making it easier for apps in gaming, design, and retail to create immersive experiences.
- **People Occlusion and Body Tracking**: ARKit's AI-driven people occlusion allows virtual objects to

interact with real-world people and objects naturally, enabling realistic and engaging AR experiences.
- **Spatial Audio and Object Detection**: ARKit uses AI to enhance spatial audio and object recognition, which is helpful for apps looking to create interactive soundscapes or detect specific objects within the AR view.

7. App Store Suggestions and Recommendations

- **Intelligent App Suggestions**: Apple's AI can suggest third-party apps in the App Store based on a user's interests, usage patterns, and activity, enhancing visibility for apps and creating a personalized discovery experience.
- **Personalized Content Recommendations**: Within Apple services like News and TV, AI curates content from third-party providers tailored to individual preferences, allowing developers to reach the most relevant audiences and keep users engaged.

8. HomeKit Integration for Smart Home Apps

- **Automated Routines and Device Control**: HomeKit allows third-party smart home apps to integrate with Apple's ecosystem, enabling automated routines, personalized schedules, and

remote device control. AI-driven insights help create energy-efficient routines and convenient automations.
- **Context-Aware Automation**: AI analyzes users' interactions with smart devices to suggest or automatically create routines, like adjusting lights, temperature, or appliances based on time of day or presence, making third-party smart home apps more intuitive and helpful.

9. Enhanced Privacy and Security with Apple's Privacy Framework

- **On-Device AI for Data Privacy**: Apple's on-device processing capabilities allow third-party apps to incorporate sophisticated AI without compromising user privacy. Sensitive data, like biometric or health information, remains on the device rather than being sent to external servers.
- **Privacy Labels and Transparency**: Apple provides privacy labels and transparency tools, so developers can clearly disclose data collection practices, earning user trust and supporting privacy-conscious app development.

10. AI Tools for Improved Accessibility

- **Accessibility Features**: Apple's AI-based accessibility tools, like VoiceOver and AssistiveTouch, are available for third-party

developers to integrate, allowing them to build apps that are more inclusive and accessible to users with disabilities.
- **Voice Control and Dictation**: Apple's AI-driven voice control allows apps to be used hands-free, benefiting users with limited mobility and creating an easier way for anyone to interact with their favorite apps through dictation and voice commands.

11. Developer Tools and AI Model Optimization

- **Model Training and Optimization**: Apple's Create ML tool lets developers train machine learning models that are optimized for Apple devices, improving performance while reducing app size and power consumption.
- **Swift and Swift Playgrounds for AI Development**: Apple offers Swift, a powerful and user-friendly language, for building and testing AI-powered apps. Swift Playgrounds further makes it accessible for developers to experiment with ML models and AI features, simplifying the process of adding AI to third-party apps.

Apple's AI support for third-party developers creates a powerful, privacy-conscious ecosystem where apps can leverage Apple's advanced machine learning and AI capabilities to deliver enhanced, personalized experiences across health, fitness, productivity, and more. This integration not only strengthens Apple's ecosystem but also offers users seamless, intelligent interactions across their favorite third-party apps

Chapter 18: Security Features and Alerts

- **Description**: How the AI strengthens security with phishing detection, suspicious link alerts, and automatic password management.

Apple's AI strengthens security across its devices and services with advanced phishing detection, suspicious link alerts, and automatic password management, helping to protect users from digital threats. Here's how Apple AI makes these security features more effective:

1. Phishing Detection and Prevention

- **Email and Message Scanning**: AI algorithms analyze email and messaging content to detect signs of phishing, like suspicious URLs, spoofed email addresses, or deceptive language patterns. By examining the structure of messages, Apple's AI can identify phishing attempts in real time and warn users before they open them.
- **Contextual Warnings for Unknown Senders**: Apple Mail and Messages use AI to differentiate between trusted and unknown senders. If a message comes from an unknown sender,

Apple's AI alerts the user, often suggesting caution with suspicious attachments or links.
- **Intelligent Link Analysis**: AI inspects URLs in messages and emails to detect potential phishing sites by analyzing link patterns, shortened URLs, or links leading to potentially dangerous sites. AI can prevent users from visiting these harmful sites, and may block such links altogether.
- **Machine Learning for Behavior Patterns**: Apple's AI uses machine learning to understand each user's typical communication behavior. If an unusual or suspicious message format or language appears, such as a financial request from an unusual contact, AI flags it as potentially harmful.

2. Suspicious Link Alerts

- **Real-Time Link Analysis in Safari**: When users click on a link, Apple's AI can analyze the destination site's metadata in real time. If the link appears unsafe—perhaps due to being flagged as malicious in a database or using deceptive practices—Safari may issue a warning or block the page entirely.
- **Enhanced Fraudulent Website Detection**: Safari uses AI-driven algorithms to detect fraudulent websites, especially those designed to look like legitimate sites. If a site looks suspicious or doesn't match typical patterns for a well-known

site, Safari alerts the user, helping prevent credential theft.
- **Cross-App Link Monitoring**: Apple's AI monitors links across apps and services, ensuring that links in emails, messages, or third-party apps are evaluated for safety. By integrating with multiple parts of the Apple ecosystem, the AI provides consistent security across all interactions involving links.

3. Automatic Password Management and Security

- **Strong Password Suggestions**: Apple's AI offers strong, randomly generated passwords when users sign up for new accounts or change existing passwords. These passwords are designed to be unique and complex, making them difficult for attackers to guess.
- **Password Reuse Warnings**: Apple's AI warns users if they reuse passwords across different sites, a common security risk. It encourages unique passwords for each account and can alert users to change reused passwords.
- **Password Monitoring for Breaches**: With its iCloud Keychain feature, Apple's AI periodically checks saved passwords against known data breaches. If a user's saved password appears in a breach, Apple notifies the user and suggests updating the password.

- **Automatic Login and Autofill**: Apple's iCloud Keychain securely stores user passwords and enables seamless login across Apple devices. This reduces the risk of phishing by ensuring users access accounts directly and securely without manually typing their credentials, especially on unfamiliar sites.
- **Two-Factor Authentication Integration**: Apple's AI also assists with the management of two-factor authentication codes. If a site supports two-factor authentication, Apple prompts users to set it up and even offers to autofill codes sent via SMS or other methods, providing added security against unauthorized access.

4. App Store and Download Security

- **App Store Review with AI**: Apple uses AI to review apps submitted to the App Store, analyzing code and behavior for potential security threats or malicious practices. This helps prevent apps with phishing or malware tendencies from being available to users.
- **Suspicious Download Alerts**: For apps downloaded outside of the App Store (for developers or enterprise use), Apple's AI checks the integrity and safety of the software. It alerts users if an app has an unknown developer or suspicious behavior, ensuring users don't unintentionally install harmful software.

5. Device-Wide Privacy Protection

- **On-Device Processing for Sensitive Data**: Many of Apple's AI-driven security features run on-device, keeping sensitive data—like message content, passwords, or personal information—secure without needing to send it to external servers. This ensures users' data remains private and less vulnerable to interception.
- **Enhanced Privacy Relay for Safe Browsing**: Apple's iCloud Private Relay anonymizes browsing activity by routing traffic through multiple servers. This limits tracking by third-party sites, reducing the chance of data interception or tracking while browsing, and prevents phishing sites from collecting personal information.

6. Behavioral Analysis for Device Security

- **AI-Driven Anomaly Detection**: Apple's AI observes typical user behavior patterns, such as location data, device unlock routines, and app usage. If AI detects unusual activity—such as a login from an unusual location or abnormal app usage—it flags this as suspicious, sometimes requiring additional authentication.
- **Find My and Device Security**: The Find My feature uses AI to monitor device location patterns and assist in securing a lost or stolen device. When a device is marked as lost, Apple AI locks it

and prevents unauthorized access, helping protect the user's personal data.

By combining on-device machine learning, real-time analysis, and privacy-first design, Apple's AI-driven security features offer a robust defense against phishing attempts, suspicious links, and password vulnerabilities. These measures empower users with proactive and accessible security while maintaining a commitment to privacy.

Chapter 19: Learning and Education Applications

- **Description**: How Apple's AI assists with educational apps, offering tutoring, reading assistance, and practice quizzes.

Apple's AI-powered features significantly enhance educational apps, providing support for tutoring, reading assistance, practice quizzes, and more. By utilizing Apple's machine learning frameworks and integrating with iOS, iPadOS, and macOS devices, educational apps can create personalized and interactive learning experiences. Here's how Apple's AI assists with educational tools:

1. Personalized Tutoring and Study Assistance

- **Adaptive Learning Models**: Apple's AI enables adaptive learning by tracking a student's progress over time and tailoring content to their learning pace and skill level. This allows educational apps to provide customized tutoring, highlighting areas where a student might need extra support and adjusting difficulty levels accordingly.
- **Real-Time Feedback and Guidance**: AI algorithms offer instant feedback on practice

exercises or assignments, providing specific suggestions or corrections. This is particularly beneficial for subjects like math and language, where step-by-step solutions help students understand concepts better.
- **Skill-Specific Tutoring**: Apple's AI can analyze areas where students struggle and recommend resources or exercises that focus on those skills. For instance, in a language app, AI might detect challenges with grammar or vocabulary and offer targeted exercises or lessons.

2. Reading Assistance and Language Support

- **Live Text Recognition and Translation**: Apple's Live Text feature, powered by AI, can recognize text within photos, scanned documents, or camera feeds in real-time. This helps students who are reading printed material or even handouts by allowing them to quickly search, translate, or look up definitions directly from the text.
- **Pronunciation Assistance with Speech Recognition**: AI-driven speech recognition helps students improve pronunciation by providing real-time feedback as they read aloud. Educational apps can leverage this to detect pronunciation errors and guide students on correct pronunciation, which is especially useful for language learning.

- **Reading Comprehension Support**: Apple's Natural Language Processing (NLP) can analyze the complexity of text and break down difficult passages, offering simplified summaries or explanations to improve comprehension. For young learners, this can mean easier vocabulary definitions, while older students can get assistance with dense or technical content.

3. Interactive Practice Quizzes and Assessments

- **Dynamic Quiz Generation**: AI can create custom practice quizzes based on a student's progress, focusing on topics they need more practice with or concepts they haven't mastered yet. This helps to reinforce learning through targeted questions and minimizes redundancy in reviewing known material.
- **Immediate Feedback with Explanations**: AI offers instant feedback on quiz answers, often including explanations or references to relevant content, so students understand their mistakes and learn correct solutions. This real-time feedback loop is helpful for mastery-based learning.
- **Gamified Learning**: AI-based adaptive learning in quizzes allows for gamification features, such as time-bound challenges, point-based scoring, and level progression, which keeps students engaged.

The AI can dynamically adjust quiz difficulty to ensure that students are both challenged and motivated.

4. Writing and Grammar Support

- **Grammar and Spell Check**: Apple's AI can analyze text for grammatical and spelling errors, offering corrections and suggestions as students type. This feature supports educational apps that focus on writing skills by providing real-time editing help and helping students develop better grammar skills.
- **Style and Tone Suggestions**: AI provides style suggestions to improve clarity, conciseness, and tone, which helps students develop better writing habits. Educational apps can give context-sensitive tips on structure, vocabulary, or sentence variety, especially for essay writing.
- **Essay Structuring Assistance**: By analyzing a draft, AI can recommend a logical structure or organization for essays or research papers. It can suggest paragraphing, transitions, and even thesis statement adjustments, making the writing process easier and more structured.

5. Math Problem-Solving and Interactive Equations

- **Equation Recognition and Solutions**: Using image recognition, educational apps can allow students to take photos of math problems, which AI then recognizes and provides solutions for. This feature helps students learn by showing step-by-step breakdowns, helping them understand the process rather than just the answer.
- **Graphing and Visualization**: For higher-level math, Apple's AI helps render graphs and visual representations of equations in real-time. Educational apps can use this to visualize complex functions or geometric shapes, aiding in conceptual understanding.
- **Interactive Practice**: AI-driven math apps can provide interactive problem-solving exercises, where students can practice a variety of problem types. The AI adapts the types of problems presented based on a student's progress, making it a highly personalized learning experience.

6. Voice Interaction and Assistance via SiriKit

- **Voice-Activated Tutoring**: Educational apps can use SiriKit to enable voice-activated tutoring, where students can ask questions and receive verbal answers or explanations. This makes learning more interactive and accessible, especially for younger children or those with reading difficulties.

- **Guided Learning Through Voice Prompts**: AI-powered voice prompts can guide students through learning activities, such as reading passages or solving problems, keeping them on task and providing assistance when needed. This is useful for hands-free learning and enables students to focus on the material rather than navigating the app.

7. Augmented Reality (AR) for Interactive Learning

- **Immersive 3D Models**: With ARKit, AI enables educational apps to offer 3D models and immersive visualizations of concepts, such as the human body, chemical structures, or historical landmarks. Students can explore these in AR, creating a more engaging and memorable learning experience.
- **Real-Time Environment Recognition**: ARKit uses AI to recognize and map real-world environments, allowing educational apps to place virtual elements in the user's surroundings. For example, students could visualize a solar system in their room or interact with virtual lab experiments, enhancing hands-on learning.
- **Interactive Experiments**: AR-enabled apps can simulate scientific experiments or historical events, enabling students to engage in learning

activities that would otherwise require specialized lab equipment or settings.

8. Time Management and Study Habit Support

- **Automated Study Scheduling**: AI analyzes a student's academic goals, deadlines, and habits to suggest study schedules and reminders. For example, if an exam is approaching, an app can remind the student to review specific topics.
- **Focus and Break Suggestions**: AI can suggest optimal study times and break intervals based on productivity patterns, helping students maintain focus without burnout. These AI-driven insights help students develop effective study routines and manage time better.

9. Real-Time Language Translation for Multi-Language Support

- **Instant Translation in Language Learning Apps**: AI-driven real-time translation capabilities allow educational apps to support students learning new languages or understanding content in non-native languages. Apple's translation tools can assist with instant translations and provide contextual understanding for words and phrases.

- **Pronunciation Feedback in Multiple Languages**: For language learners, AI-powered pronunciation feedback in various languages helps students improve their accents and fluency, making it easier to learn and retain new language skills.

10. Data-Driven Progress Tracking and Analytics

- **Individualized Progress Reports**: Apple's AI helps generate detailed progress reports based on a student's learning activities, showing strengths, weaknesses, and trends over time. Educational apps can present this data in visual formats, allowing students, parents, and educators to easily track academic growth.
- **Goal Setting and Achievement Tracking**: AI enables students to set goals within educational apps, like mastering a certain number of vocabulary words per week, and track their progress. The AI can adjust activities to help students meet these goals and celebrate milestones, keeping them motivated.
- **Predictive Analytics for Success**: AI can analyze a student's progress to predict their future performance or the likelihood of mastering a concept. This is helpful for teachers and parents, as they can intervene and provide support if the

data suggests a student may struggle with upcoming material.

11. Accessibility Features for Inclusive Education

- **Assistive Tools for Students with Disabilities**: Apple's AI accessibility tools, such as VoiceOver, text-to-speech, and AssistiveTouch, make educational apps more accessible. For instance, visually impaired students can use text-to-speech, while those with physical disabilities can use voice-activated controls to navigate content.
- **Learning Mode Adjustments**: AI-driven settings can allow educational apps to adapt to different learning styles. For example, AI can recognize when a student responds better to visual content and adjust the presentation of material accordingly.

Apple's AI technology, integrated with its ecosystem of frameworks and developer tools, provides educational app creators with the resources to create supportive, engaging, and personalized learning experiences for students of all ages and learning styles

Chapter 20: AI-Driven Language Translation and Learning

- **Description**: Translation capabilities and real-time language practice powered by Apple's AI.

Apple's AI enhances language translation and real-time language practice by using machine learning for fast, accurate translation and interactive language learning experiences. These AI-driven language capabilities support users in daily communication, travel, education, and practice within a seamless, on-device framework. Here's an overview of how Apple's AI powers translation and language practice:

1. Real-Time Translation with Apple Translate

- **Instant Text and Voice Translation**: Apple's Translate app, powered by AI, provides fast, real-time translations for both text and voice. Users can translate conversations across multiple languages simply by speaking or typing, and AI processes the translations quickly to support natural, ongoing conversations.
- **On-Device Processing for Privacy**: Translations are processed on-device (for supported languages), which protects user privacy by

keeping data secure and offline. This is particularly useful in scenarios where users may need translations in private or sensitive conversations.
- **Automatic Language Detection**: Apple's AI can automatically detect the language being spoken or typed, switching between languages seamlessly. This helps maintain the flow of conversations without needing manual adjustments, especially in multilingual settings.

2. Text Recognition and Translation with Live Text

- **Real-Time Text Recognition**: Apple's Live Text feature, supported by AI, allows users to capture text from physical items, such as signs, documents, or labels, using the camera. Live Text recognizes and translates text directly in the camera view, making it easy to understand foreign languages in real-world contexts.
- **Instant Translation on Photos and Screenshots**: Users can take a photo of text in a foreign language, and Live Text will extract and translate it immediately. This is particularly useful for travelers and students, who can get on-the-spot translations for information on restaurant menus, instruction manuals, or product labels.

3. Pronunciation Assistance and Real-Time Language Practice

- **Pronunciation Feedback**: Apple's speech recognition and AI-driven pronunciation tools allow users to practice speaking in a new language. The AI listens to pronunciation and offers real-time feedback, helping users improve accuracy and build confidence when speaking.
- **Interactive Conversations with Siri**: Users can practice language skills with Siri by asking questions or using conversational commands in the target language. Siri's AI processes responses in the selected language, providing both practice opportunities and contextually relevant responses, enhancing real-time conversational skills.
- **Phrase Suggestions and Contextual Learning**: AI-driven language suggestions in the Translate app help users learn phrases commonly used in the context of their translations, reinforcing vocabulary and offering situational learning, such as travel or business phrases.

4. Support for Multilingual Users Across Apple Ecosystem

- **Keyboard Support and Predictive Text**: Apple's AI offers multilingual predictive text, auto-correction, and language switching based on

context. This is helpful for bilingual or multilingual users who switch languages frequently, as the keyboard can automatically adjust and provide language-specific suggestions.
- **Quick Language Switching**: In both Translate and Siri, AI enables smooth transitions between languages without interrupting the flow. Users can switch languages during translations or conversations, allowing bilingual communication without the need for repetitive adjustments.
- **Offline Translation for Accessibility**: Apple's Translate app supports offline translation in several languages, which makes it accessible in areas with limited connectivity. This offline capability ensures that users have reliable language assistance whenever and wherever needed.

5. Enhanced Language Learning and Vocabulary Building

- **Context-Aware Translations and Definitions**: Apple's AI provides translations that take into account the context and nuances of words, offering definitions, examples, and alternative translations. This is particularly useful for language learners who need to understand variations in meaning.
- **Bilingual Dictionary Integration**: Apple integrates bilingual dictionaries directly into the

Translate app, allowing users to tap on individual words to see detailed meanings, synonyms, and grammatical information. This helps users deepen their understanding of vocabulary in context.
- **Phrasebook for Personalized Practice**: Users can save frequently used or favorite phrases in the Translate app's phrasebook, which is powered by AI to suggest relevant phrases based on previous translations. This feature acts as a personalized language guide, helping users review and practice specific phrases over time.

6. Accessibility and Inclusivity in Language Translation

- **Voice Accessibility for Users with Disabilities**: Apple's voice-driven language tools help users with disabilities engage in real-time translation and practice. Voice commands, Siri, and text-to-speech options allow users to interact with translations and language content without needing to type.
- **Translation Across Apple Devices**: With cross-device support, users can access Apple's translation capabilities on iPhone, iPad, Mac, and Apple Watch, ensuring language assistance is available across all their Apple devices.

7. Augmented Reality Language Assistance with ARKit

- **AR Translations in Real-World Context**: Apple's AI and ARKit can work together to provide real-time translations in an augmented reality environment, making foreign text visible with translations overlaid in real-world locations. This can be helpful for reading signs, historical information, or instructions in foreign languages during travel.

Apple's AI-powered translation and language practice capabilities deliver intuitive, reliable, and privacy-focused language support across various contexts. Whether users are learning a new language, traveling, or communicating with speakers of other languages, Apple's AI provides seamless, real-time language assistance that adapts to individual needs and settings.

Chapter 21: Tips for Efficient AI Use on iOS 18.2

- **Description**: Tips and tricks for users to optimize AI features for productivity and efficiency.

Here are some practical tips for using AI on iOS 18.2 to its fullest potential:

1. Optimize Siri for Productivity

- **Use Custom Shortcuts**: Set up Siri Shortcuts to automate common tasks, like sending quick messages, adjusting smart home settings, or even starting a workout. This allows Siri to perform multi-step actions with a single command, streamlining routines.
- **Leverage Contextual Suggestions**: Siri now provides smarter contextual reminders and suggestions. For instance, if you missed a call or email, Siri can suggest a follow-up. Enable Siri Suggestions in Settings > Siri & Search for the most useful AI-driven recommendations.

2. Improve Focus with Adaptive Focus Modes

- **Smart Focus Filters**: In iOS 18.2, Focus modes have smarter filters for notifications, allowing you to selectively silence non-essential alerts. Customize Focus modes for specific activities like work, study, or sleep to improve productivity and reduce distractions.
- **Location and Time-Based Activations**: Set Focus modes to automatically activate based on location or time. For example, automatically switching to a work Focus when you arrive at your office keeps you focused with minimal setup.

3. Enhance Privacy and Security with AI Tools

- **Use Safari's Intelligent Tracking Prevention**: Enable this feature in Safari settings to reduce tracking by third-party websites. Safari's AI can prevent cross-site trackers from following you while still allowing you to browse smoothly.
- **Enable Suspicious Link Detection**: For added security, turn on link previews in Safari. This will help identify phishing attempts or suspicious links by displaying website previews before you visit them.

4. Maximize Photos App's AI Tools

- **Explore Memories and People Album**: Photos now organizes pictures more intelligently, so

review Memories and the People album regularly to rediscover important moments. You can also adjust which faces and events Photos AI highlights.
- **Leverage Live Text for Instant Info**: Use Live Text to extract information from images, such as addresses or phone numbers, and save them directly to contacts or calendars. This makes it easy to interact with text in photos without retyping.

5. Use AI-Powered Translation for Language Practice

- **Practice with Real-Time Translation**: For language learners, the Translate app now supports real-time feedback and pronunciation. Try speaking phrases and let Translate provide corrections and suggestions for more immersive learning.
- **Enable Auto-Detect for Seamless Switching**: Enable automatic language detection in the Translate app for smoother conversations. This will automatically recognize and translate both languages without needing to manually switch.

6. Boost Health and Fitness Tracking with AI Insights

- **Check Out New Sleep and Wellness Insights**: In iOS 18.2, Apple Health offers deeper insights into sleep quality, heart rate variability, and wellness trends. Set up your Health app preferences to receive personalized recommendations for healthier habits.
- **Utilize Real-Time Fitness Coaching**: AI on Apple Watch can now provide live feedback during workouts. Use this feature to adjust your form, pace, or intensity for safer, more effective exercise.

7. Smart Home Automation in HomeKit

- **Set Up Automated Routines**: With iOS 18.2, Apple's AI suggests smart home routines like turning off lights when you leave or adjusting the thermostat at bedtime. Use the "Suggested Automations" in the Home app to simplify setup.
- **Energy Efficiency Insights**: HomeKit now provides tips for energy efficiency, like when to turn off unused devices or adjust thermostat settings to save on energy costs. Check the Energy usage reports within the Home app.

8. Explore Customization and Personalization

- **Widgets and Smart Stacks**: Add Smart Stacks of widgets that use AI to show relevant information

throughout the day. This could include traffic, calendar events, or weather updates, all personalized to your habits and preferences.
- **Personalize Content in News and Music**: Use the AI-powered recommendation engine in Apple News and Music to discover new content. Mark stories, genres, or artists you enjoy to help Apple's algorithms improve your future recommendations.

9. Use Notes and Reminders with AI Suggestions

- **Quick Notes Suggestions**: The Notes app can now suggest related notes or highlight key points from recent entries. Use these suggestions to find relevant notes quickly and stay organized.
- **Reminder Suggestions Based on Context**: Reminders can now suggest tasks based on location or time context. This means you'll get nudges about items you may want to add based on recent activities or locations, like a grocery list reminder near a store.

10. Privacy and Security Enhancements in Password Management

- **Use Password Monitoring**: iOS 18.2 offers enhanced password security with alerts about

compromised passwords. Enable this feature in Settings > Passwords to receive alerts and quickly change at-risk credentials.
- **Two-Factor Code Autofill**: Enable two-factor authentication (2FA) for supported apps and websites to add an extra layer of security. iOS 18.2 now autofills 2FA codes from SMS, streamlining the login process.

11. Productivity Tips for Safari and Search

- **Search Shortcuts in Safari**: Add custom search engines in Safari for quicker access to specific sites. AI-powered search suggestions help you find relevant sites and content based on browsing history.
- **Enhanced Visual Search with Spotlight**: Use Spotlight to search for photos, documents, or content across apps. AI allows Spotlight to categorize images based on elements within them, making it easier to locate specific visuals.

Following these tips, you'll be able to leverage Apple's AI capabilities on iOS 18.2 for enhanced productivity, smarter device management, and a more personalized experience tailored to your needs.

Chapter 22: A Comparison with Other Mobile AI Assistants

- **Description**: A comparative look at Apple's AI versus other smartphone assistants, highlighting strengths and differences.

Apple's AI, particularly through Siri and the broader iOS ecosystem, has unique strengths and differences when compared to other smartphone assistants like Google Assistant, Samsung's Bixby, and Amazon's Alexa. Here's a comparative look at how Apple's AI stacks up:

1. Privacy and On-Device Processing

- **Apple's Strength**: Privacy is a central focus for Apple, and its AI typically processes data on-device rather than in the cloud. Siri's requests for certain tasks are handled on the device, minimizing the amount of data shared with Apple's servers, particularly for sensitive actions like messaging, photos, or location-based reminders.
- **Competitors**: Google Assistant and Alexa often rely heavily on cloud processing, allowing them to aggregate more data for training and broader functionality but at the cost of more data collection. Google has recently added on-device

processing to the Pixel line for select tasks, but generally, its model relies on server-side AI processing. Bixby is similar, providing voice assistance with cloud processing but less emphasis on privacy compared to Apple.

2. Integration with Ecosystem

- **Apple's Strength**: Apple's AI is seamlessly integrated across all Apple devices, from iPhone to Apple Watch, Mac, and Apple TV. This tight integration means that Siri and Apple's AI features offer continuity across devices with features like Handoff, Universal Clipboard, and personalized recommendations in apps like Safari, Photos, and Health.
- **Competitors**: Google Assistant is highly integrated within Google's own ecosystem (Android phones, Chromebooks, Google Home devices) and has an edge in the broader smart home space. Alexa, while also versatile across devices, is primarily focused on smart home control and is less focused on the mobile experience. Bixby's ecosystem integration is limited mainly to Samsung devices and doesn't offer as consistent an experience across devices as Apple or Google.

3. Functionality and Versatility

- **Apple's Strength**: Siri is known for performing basic tasks very well—calling, sending messages, setting reminders, and controlling Apple devices—while remaining focused on enhancing user privacy. Siri also supports complex multi-step routines with Siri Shortcuts, allowing users to automate sequences across different apps and devices.
- **Competitors**: Google Assistant generally surpasses Siri in task complexity, context awareness, and natural conversation flow. For example, Google Assistant can understand follow-up questions and commands in a more conversational style and can perform more complex tasks within the Google ecosystem, like reading emails or interacting directly with Google Workspace. Alexa, optimized for smart home controls, leads in supporting third-party smart devices but is more limited on mobile devices. Bixby, while improving, is often viewed as less intuitive and doesn't match the versatility of Siri or Google Assistant.

4. Context Awareness and Personalization

- **Apple's Strength**: Siri has gained contextual abilities with each update, offering suggestions based on time, location, and usage patterns across apps. For example, Siri can suggest reminders based on missed calls or automatically

create calendar events from emails. Apple's Focus modes and notification suggestions further personalize the experience based on user context.
- **Competitors**: Google Assistant leads in contextual awareness, using Google's extensive data and AI training to offer more accurate, personalized responses. For example, it can answer follow-up questions based on a prior response, engage in multi-turn conversations, and suggest personalized content based on search and browsing history. Alexa has limited context awareness on mobile but performs well in routines and household commands. Bixby offers some contextual suggestions but isn't as nuanced or developed in this area.

5. Smart Home Capabilities

- **Apple's Strength**: Apple's HomeKit ecosystem is private and secure, with end-to-end encryption for HomeKit-compatible devices. Apple's AI suggests automations based on device usage, location, and time of day, such as setting routines for lights or climate control. Siri's smart home control is straightforward and integrates seamlessly with Apple's hardware.
- **Competitors**: Alexa has the largest smart home ecosystem, offering the broadest device compatibility and more advanced automation

options. Google Assistant is also strong here, with wide compatibility and routines that integrate seamlessly with Nest products. Bixby offers smart home control primarily through Samsung's SmartThings ecosystem, which, while comprehensive, lacks the widespread support of Google or Alexa.

6. Natural Language Processing and Voice Recognition

- **Apple's Strength**: Siri's natural language processing has improved significantly, especially in newer updates, with better understanding of nuanced phrases and a more natural voice response. It handles straightforward requests reliably and has expanded vocabulary and language support.
- **Competitors**: Google Assistant is often considered the most advanced in understanding natural language and contextual follow-up questions, making it highly responsive in conversational settings. Alexa also performs well in language processing, particularly for handling routines and voice commands in the smart home setting. Bixby's language processing has improved but is generally more limited in conversational abilities than Siri, Google Assistant, or Alexa.

7. Third-Party Integration and Developer Support

- **Apple's Strength**: Apple allows third-party developers to create Siri Shortcuts, but integration is typically limited compared to Google and Alexa. However, Shortcuts offer robust automation possibilities, letting users set up customized workflows that involve third-party apps.
- **Competitors**: Google Assistant and Alexa have extensive third-party support, allowing more direct integration into apps and devices. Alexa is particularly strong here, offering thousands of third-party "skills" that extend its functionality in the smart home and beyond. Google also supports third-party commands for a wider range of actions, enhancing user experience on Android. Bixby's marketplace is smaller, with fewer third-party integrations, and doesn't provide as much customization.

8. Language and Localization Support

- **Apple's Strength**: Siri is available in over 20 languages with regional dialect support, and Apple prioritizes providing localized experiences tailored to specific regions. This includes localized suggestions and search results that align with user preferences and location.

- **Competitors**: Google Assistant supports over 30 languages with strong localization, and its natural language understanding is more advanced, which makes it particularly useful for multi-language users. Alexa also offers support in multiple languages but is focused more on smart home commands rather than broader, nuanced language support. Bixby supports fewer languages and is generally limited in localization features.

9. Privacy and Security Features

- **Apple's Strength**: Apple stands out in privacy, ensuring minimal data collection and providing transparency about AI usage. Siri is designed to operate with on-device processing whenever possible, and Apple's strict privacy guidelines make Siri the preferred choice for privacy-conscious users.
- **Competitors**: Google Assistant and Alexa rely more on data collection to improve personalization and functionality, which can raise privacy concerns. Google and Amazon both allow users to review and delete recorded interactions, but they still depend heavily on cloud data. Bixby, while less intrusive, also doesn't prioritize privacy as strongly as Apple.

10. Learning and Adaptability

- **Apple's Strength**: Siri has shown steady improvement in learning user preferences, especially with the introduction of Siri Suggestions and Shortcuts. It now adapts more to individual use patterns across apps and devices, suggesting actions based on repeated behaviors.
- **Competitors**: Google Assistant's adaptability is industry-leading due to its deep integration with Google's vast data sets. It can anticipate user needs more effectively, often suggesting content, reminders, and answers before the user asks. Alexa also learns from user interactions, especially within the smart home, but its adaptability is more confined to device-specific routines. Bixby offers limited adaptability and hasn't reached the sophistication of Siri or Google Assistant in this area.

In Summary

Apple's AI, especially in iOS and Siri, prioritizes privacy, seamless ecosystem integration, and security, making it ideal for users who value these elements. Google Assistant generally leads in intelligence, contextual awareness, and natural language processing, while Alexa excels in smart home control and third-party support. Each assistant has strengths tailored to different user preferences:

- **Apple's Siri**: Ideal for privacy-focused users invested in Apple's ecosystem, providing reliable functionality with a strong emphasis on privacy and security.
- **Google Assistant**: Best for users who need advanced context-awareness, conversational interaction, and strong Google integration.
- **Amazon Alexa**: Best for smart home enthusiasts who want extensive third-party device support and customizations.
- **Samsung Bixby**: Primarily for Samsung users who want device control and prefer Samsung's ecosystem but with limited functionality outside it.

Ultimately, Apple's AI may not always match the complexity of Google Assistant or Alexa, but it provides a highly secure, reliable, and increasingly adaptable assistant within its ecosystem.

Chapter 23: User Feedback on iOS 18.2 Beta AI

- **Description**: Summary of beta user reviews and their insights on new AI features, gathered from early adopters

Early user feedback on Apple's new AI features in iOS 18.2 is largely positive, with beta testers highlighting both strengths and areas for improvement. Many users praise the enhanced Siri, which now offers a more conversational experience and the ability to understand complex, natural language requests. Siri can guide users through tasks, link to Apple Support for troubleshooting, and even make navigating iPhone settings more user-friendly. This update improves accessibility and tech support for users unfamiliar with advanced device features.

In the Photos app, Apple's AI has introduced more powerful search capabilities, allowing users to search for specific objects or scenes using natural language. Although this feature occasionally misidentifies objects, testers report that it effectively finds relevant images among large photo libraries. Additionally, features like automated sorting and duplicate detection make organizing photos much easier.

Apple's AI also includes call transcription and summarization, a feature beta users find valuable, especially for summarizing important points from conversations. While the transcription quality is mostly accurate, it may sometimes misinterpret certain words based on accents or context. Users hope for improved accuracy and integration with the Phone app for easier access.

In general, early adopters appreciate the convenience and added value Apple's AI brings to daily tasks, even if some features are still being fine-tuned for accuracy and consistency. Overall, users look forward to seeing these AI-driven improvements reach full maturity as Apple continues to refine them.

Chapter 24: Real-Life Scenarios: AI's Daily Benefits

- **Description**: Illustrative scenarios on how users can benefit from Apple's AI in everyday life.

Apple's AI enhancements can greatly improve users' everyday lives in numerous practical and personalized ways. Here are some scenarios where Apple's AI can make a difference:

1. Streamlining Daily Routines

- **Example**: A user sets up AI-powered Siri Shortcuts for their morning routine. With one command, Siri could automate actions like turning on the bedroom lights, reading the day's weather, opening the calendar to check appointments, and even starting a playlist for their commute.
- **Benefit**: By using Siri Shortcuts, the user saves time and can transition smoothly into their day with minimal effort.

2. Enhanced Health and Fitness Monitoring

- **Example**: A fitness enthusiast uses Apple's Health app with AI-driven suggestions to optimize workouts. The app could analyze the user's activity trends and suggest personalized workout

routines, or remind them to rest based on heart rate data or sleep patterns.
- **Benefit**: This makes workout planning easier and more effective, helping users reach fitness goals safely and efficiently.

3. Improving Work Efficiency

- **Example**: A user in a remote work setting uses the AI call transcription and summarization feature to keep track of meeting points. After a lengthy call, they can review the AI-generated summary in the Notes app, catching important action items without having to re-listen to the entire conversation.
- **Benefit**: This saves significant time, allowing the user to focus on actionable points without the hassle of manual note-taking during calls.

4. Smart Photo Organization for Memories

- **Example**: A parent looking for photos of a specific family trip can simply type a natural language query like "beach trip with kids" in the Photos app. The AI recognizes specific scenes, people, and places, making it easier to find exact moments from thousands of images.
- **Benefit**: This feature transforms photo browsing from a lengthy, manual process into a quick, AI-

assisted experience, helping users relive special moments instantly.

5. Enhanced Privacy and Security Management

- **Example**: A user frequently receives links and attachments in emails and texts. Apple's AI analyzes these in real time, flagging any suspicious links or phishing attempts, and automatically suggests strong passwords for online accounts.
- **Benefit**: This adds a layer of protection, especially for users who are not always aware of cybersecurity best practices. AI can reduce the risk of security breaches by actively monitoring and alerting users to potential threats.

6. Multilingual Communication and Travel Assistance

- **Example**: While traveling, a user can access Apple's real-time translation capabilities in iOS. They can speak a phrase in English, and Siri translates it aloud in the local language, helping them navigate interactions with locals, order food, or get directions.
- **Benefit**: Real-time translation makes international travel smoother and bridges communication

barriers, giving users confidence to interact in different languages.

7. Personalized Learning for Students

- **Example**: A student uses Apple's AI for studying, with interactive suggestions for practice quizzes and custom learning resources based on topics they're struggling with. Siri can assist with complex math problems or even provide reading assistance for language learning.
- **Benefit**: This individualized approach to learning helps students focus on weak areas and makes self-study more efficient, reinforcing their education outside the classroom.

8. Smart Home Automation for Convenience and Energy Efficiency

- **Example**: A user sets up a HomeKit automation that recognizes when they arrive home and triggers specific actions: lights turn on, the thermostat adjusts, and their favorite playlist starts. The AI could also suggest energy-saving routines based on household behavior, such as turning off unnecessary lights.
- **Benefit**: AI-powered automations create a seamless, customized home experience and can even lead to energy savings over time.

Apple's AI features thus enhance productivity, security, health, and leisure, while also adapting to each user's unique lifestyle and preferences, making everyday tasks smoother and more efficient.

Chapter 25: Developers and Apple's AI Ecosystem

- **Description**: How developers can leverage Apple's new AI features in their apps, supported by Apple's developer tools

Apple's new AI features offer developers robust tools to enhance their apps, allowing for more personalized, efficient, and intuitive user experiences. Through Apple's developer tools, such as Core ML, Vision, Natural Language, and Create ML, developers can integrate advanced machine learning capabilities directly into their apps. Here's how they can leverage these features:

1. Enhanced Image Recognition and Processing with Core ML and Vision

- **How It Works**: Core ML enables developers to use Apple's machine learning models for image analysis, object recognition, and even photo categorization. For example, the Vision framework allows developers to analyze images and videos, recognize objects, and apply real-time effects.
- **Developer Use**: An app focused on retail or fashion can use Vision to let users take photos of products and immediately see related items in

stock. Similarly, a fitness app could use real-time pose estimation to guide users on exercise form.
- **Benefits**: Leveraging these tools enables developers to provide more interactive, visual experiences. With the Vision API's efficiency on Apple's neural engine, these features run smoothly on device, ensuring privacy and speed.

2. Natural Language Processing (NLP) for Contextual Understanding

- **How It Works**: Apple's Natural Language framework allows apps to understand and process text more intelligently, enabling features like sentiment analysis, language translation, and summarization. Developers can use this framework to analyze text input from users, detect intent, and respond accordingly.
- **Developer Use**: Messaging and social media apps can use NLP to filter out spam or inappropriate content, offer text predictions, or suggest relevant replies. Education apps might offer reading assistance by summarizing paragraphs or identifying key terms.
- **Benefits**: By utilizing Apple's NLP tools, developers can create apps that understand user input in a more human-like way, making interactions feel more natural and intuitive.

3. Personalization and Predictive Features with Create ML

- **How It Works**: Create ML offers tools for developers to train machine learning models on-device, which means apps can adapt to user behavior over time without sharing data with third parties. Models can be created for personalized content recommendations, predictive text, or habit tracking.
- **Developer Use**: Health and wellness apps can offer customized workout plans by analyzing users' activity trends. News apps might suggest articles based on reading history and preferences, while productivity tools can prioritize tasks based on user habits.
- **Benefits**: By training models on device, developers provide a more private, customized experience, aligning with Apple's focus on user privacy and reducing dependency on external data sources.

4. Real-time Translation and Speech Recognition

- **How It Works**: Using Apple's Speech and Translation APIs, developers can integrate real-time language translation and transcription capabilities. The translation API supports text and

speech translation between multiple languages, while speech recognition enables transcription of spoken input.
- **Developer Use**: Language-learning apps can offer real-time conversation practice, while travel apps can include a translation feature for navigating foreign environments. Apps for productivity can include voice dictation features, turning spoken commands into actionable tasks.
- **Benefits**: These features open up opportunities for accessibility and global reach, allowing developers to build apps that support multiple languages and diverse user needs.

5. Privacy-Focused Data Handling

- **How It Works**: Apple's machine learning frameworks emphasize on-device processing and differential privacy, allowing developers to build secure and private apps.
- **Developer Use**: Health or financial apps, for example, can process sensitive data directly on the device, minimizing data sent to external servers and enhancing user trust.
- **Benefits**: Developers can use Apple's privacy-centric tools to meet user expectations around data security, a competitive advantage in an increasingly privacy-conscious market.

6. Seamless Integration with Apple's Ecosystem

- **How It Works**: Developers can leverage Apple's ecosystem-wide integration for apps that sync across iPhone, iPad, Mac, Apple Watch, and HomeKit. With Siri Shortcuts, developers can create voice commands to trigger specific actions in their apps, making them more accessible and easy to use.
- **Developer Use**: A smart home app can allow users to create Siri shortcuts to control their devices. A to-do list app could set up Siri reminders or add tasks to the calendar.
- **Benefits**: By utilizing Siri and Apple's other ecosystem features, developers make their apps more useful across Apple devices, enhancing user loyalty and engagement.

Summary

Apple's AI features empower developers to create apps that are smarter, more responsive, and more personalized. By integrating tools like Core ML, Vision, and Create ML, developers can offer sophisticated capabilities, from image recognition to natural language processing, all while respecting user privacy

.

Chapter 26: How AI in iOS 18.2 Impacts Battery Life

- **Description**: Explanation of how Apple has optimized AI usage to maintain battery efficiency.

In iOS 18.2, Apple has integrated new AI-driven features across various functions, which could have both positive and negative impacts on battery life, depending on how they are managed. Here's an overview of how AI affects battery performance:

1. On-Device Processing

- Apple's AI models primarily run on-device, using the Neural Engine and custom machine learning frameworks (like Core ML). By avoiding cloud-based data processing, Apple can reduce latency and preserve user privacy while optimizing energy consumption. The use of the Neural Engine, which is designed to handle ML tasks efficiently, ensures that high-demand AI functions like image recognition, natural language processing, and predictive text can run without taxing the battery as much as a general-purpose processor might.

2. Adaptive Power Management

- iOS 18.2 includes adaptive power management that dynamically allocates resources to AI features only when they're actively needed. For example, if a user's iPhone is idle or in a low-power mode, AI tasks like continuous background analysis (such as Siri suggestions or background app refreshing) are minimized to conserve battery. This optimization helps balance power usage by running AI functions only when they're likely to be beneficial to the user.

3. Battery Saver Integration for AI Functions

- When Low Power Mode is enabled, iOS 18.2 limits background AI tasks, including real-time transcription, certain Siri functionalities, and background updates from Photos' image recognition processes. This intentional throttling allows users to benefit from the AI enhancements without excessive battery drain.

4. Impact of Intensive Features on Battery Life

- Some AI features, especially those that require real-time data processing, can be battery-intensive. For example, live transcription or real-time translation requires continuous processing, which can lead to higher power consumption during prolonged use. Users have reported that these features are best used sparingly or with the device connected to power for extended sessions, such as during long conversations or language practice.

5. Optimizations for Location-Based AI Features

- iOS 18.2 also makes location-based AI smarter in terms of energy usage. Features like automated Siri suggestions based on location or context use less power by optimizing GPS usage, thereby reducing the need for constant location tracking. This helps extend battery life, especially for users who frequently rely on location-specific features.

6. User Control Over AI Features

- iOS 18.2 allows users to manage AI feature settings more directly. This includes enabling or disabling AI-driven background tasks in Settings, letting users choose which features they find most useful versus those they may not need frequently. Turning off features like Siri suggestions, Photos analysis, or Background App Refresh can help preserve battery for users prioritizing battery life over AI-driven convenience.

Overall, Apple's AI in iOS 18.2 is designed with battery efficiency in mind, utilizing specialized hardware, power management, and user control options. Users who want to conserve battery life have options to limit or disable more intensive AI features, while those who prioritize smart functionality can leverage these new tools without excessive power drain.

Chapter 27: The Future of AI in Apple's Ecosystem

- **Description**: Speculation on future AI advancements in iOS based on current trends and Apple's investment in AI.

The future of AI in Apple's ecosystem is poised for significant growth and refinement, with Apple focusing on creating a seamless, secure, and user-friendly experience across its range of devices. A key strategy for Apple is its **on-device AI** capabilities, which prioritize user privacy by processing data locally rather than relying on cloud-based servers. This ensures that users' data stays secure, with minimal risk of breaches, while still allowing for powerful, real-time AI processing

Aragon Research

AppleInsider

.

Looking ahead, **Apple Intelligence**, set to expand significantly in iOS 18 and beyond, will continue to enhance productivity, creativity, and communication through advanced features like **Siri 2.0**, more sophisticated content generation tools (e.g., for text and images), and smarter task automation across devices

Counterpoint Research

. The **AI-driven App Intents** framework will allow deeper integration of AI into Apple's ecosystem, enabling apps to leverage Apple's advanced AI models for more intuitive interactions

Counterpoint Research

.

Chapter 28: Addressing AI Misconceptions and Fears

- **Description**: Discuss common myths around AI and clarify Apple's stance on responsible AI.

There are several myths surrounding Artificial Intelligence (AI) that can cloud public understanding. Apple, as a leader in integrating AI into its ecosystem, has made its stance on responsible AI clear. Here's a breakdown of some common myths and how Apple addresses them through its focus on ethical AI:

Myth 1: AI Will Eventually Replace Human Jobs Completely

- **Reality**: While AI is expected to automate certain tasks, it is not designed to replace humans entirely. Rather, it can complement human abilities, enhancing productivity and allowing people to focus on more creative, strategic tasks. For instance, Apple's AI features, like Siri and AI-driven suggestions, are designed to assist users, not replace their roles. Apple's approach

emphasizes **collaboration** between humans and AI, rather than displacement.
- **Apple's Stance**: Apple focuses on **empowering users** with AI tools to enhance their work, from creative endeavors (e.g., photo editing) to improving efficiency in daily tasks (e.g., personal assistants). AI is meant to support and not replace human interaction
AppleInsider
.

Myth 2: AI Is Unbiased and Always Reliable

- **Reality**: AI systems are only as good as the data they are trained on. If the data is biased, the AI system will also reflect those biases. Apple is conscious of this challenge and works to ensure its AI models are as unbiased as possible.
- **Apple's Stance**: Apple places a strong emphasis on **responsible AI** by ensuring that its models are trained on diverse, representative datasets. Moreover, Apple's commitment to **privacy** plays a key role in making AI systems more transparent and accountable. On-device AI helps minimize risks related to bias and ensures better user control
Counterpoint Research

AppleInsider
.

Myth 3: AI Can Surpass Human Intelligence (Superintelligence)

- **Reality**: AI, even with advanced capabilities like machine learning and deep learning, operates within narrowly defined boundaries. It excels at specific tasks but lacks **general intelligence** or the ability to think and reason in the broad, nuanced way that humans can. AI cannot "think" or possess consciousness.
- **Apple's Stance**: Apple's approach to AI is grounded in **human-centric design**. The goal is not to create a superintelligent system, but to develop tools that improve people's lives without exceeding ethical limits. For instance, Siri and other AI features are designed to assist, not to take over decision-making or perform general reasoning
  [AppleInsider](#)
  .

Myth 4: AI Needs Massive Amounts of Data to Be Effective

- **Reality**: While large datasets can improve the performance of AI models, effective AI can also be built using smaller, well-curated datasets. Additionally, AI systems can be designed to learn from interactions without needing vast amounts of

data. **Privacy** is a key concern, and Apple has ensured that many AI functions are **on-device**, meaning data does not need to be uploaded to servers for processing.
- **Apple's Stance**: Apple's focus on **on-device AI** reduces the need for extensive data collection, ensuring user privacy. Data processing occurs directly on the device, which is in line with Apple's commitment to ethical, **user-controlled data** management
AppleInsider

Myth 5: AI Will Compromise User Privacy

- **Reality**: Concerns about privacy and AI often stem from the fear of personal data being misused. While many AI systems rely on cloud computing and external data storage, Apple's AI operates differently.
- **Apple's Stance**: Apple has made privacy a cornerstone of its AI initiatives. AI tasks like Siri voice recognition, predictive text, and image classification are processed on-device rather than in the cloud. Apple's **differential privacy** approach ensures that individual user data is not identifiable or used for targeted advertising. Apple's commitment to **privacy-first AI** ensures that AI is used responsibly and transparently
Aragon Research

AppleInsider.

Myth 6: AI Is Only Useful for Tech-Savvy Users

- **Reality**: Many people assume AI is too complex or technical for everyday users. In reality, AI-powered features like voice assistants, smart photo management, and predictive text are already making devices more intuitive and user-friendly.
- **Apple's Stance**: Apple integrates AI seamlessly into the everyday experience. From the user-friendly interface of Siri to AI-driven suggestions in the Photos app, Apple ensures that AI is accessible, simple, and enhances user experience across all levels of technical knowledge
AppleInsider.

Conclusion: Apple's Ethical AI Vision

Apple's approach to AI centers on responsible use and **human-centric design**. While myths about AI abound, Apple's emphasis on **privacy**, **security**, and **bias reduction** positions it as a leader in the ethical use of AI technologies. By ensuring that AI enhances user experience without compromising privacy or ethical standards, Apple paves the way for a more transparent and trustworthy AI future.

Chapter 29: Expert Opinions on iOS 18.2's AI

- **Description**: Insights from AI and tech experts about iOS 18.2's new features, with possible pros and cons.

Experts have shared various opinions on the new AI features introduced in iOS 18.2, highlighting both positive innovations and areas of concern.

Pros:

1. **Enhanced Siri Capabilities**: The integration of ChatGPT into Siri allows for more accurate and nuanced responses, especially when Siri encounters questions it cannot answer directly. This makes Siri a much more versatile assistant [The Mac Observer](#).

2. **Apple Intelligence**: With tools like Image Playground, Genmoji, and Visual Intelligence, Apple has taken strides toward making its ecosystem more interactive and creative. Users can generate images based on text descriptions and create customizable emojis, expanding the ways in which AI can enhance communication [The Mac Observer](#).

[9to5Mac](#)

3. **Security and Privacy Focus**: Apple continues to prioritize user safety and data privacy, with responsible AI practices that limit potential misuse of image-generation tools. The company implements a waitlist for new features to ensure proper functioning before widespread release [9to5Mac](#)

Cons:

1. **Feature Access Delays**: While the new AI tools are impressive, they are not immediately accessible to all users. A waitlist system has been implemented for features like Image Playground and Genmoji, which can be frustrating for those eager to explore these innovations [9to5Mac](#)

2. **Learning Curve**: As these features grow, some users may find the AI capabilities complex, particularly with the integration of visual intelligence and AI-driven content creation tools [The Mac Observer](#)

3. **Battery and Performance Concerns**: Some users have noted that the AI features could potentially strain battery life or performance,

especially in older devices. While Apple claims that its AI optimizations are efficient, real-world testing will be crucial to assess their long-term impact

[The Mac Observer](#)
.

Overall, experts generally view iOS 18.2 as a leap forward in AI integration, with the potential to significantly improve user experience. However, Apple's careful rollout and focus on user feedback reflect a commitment to addressing the challenges that come with such advanced features.

Chapter 30: Getting the Most Out of iOS 18.2 AI: A Summary

- **Description**: Summarized tips, features, and insights for users looking to make the most of iOS 18.2's AI.

Here's a summary of tips, features, and insights to help you make the most of iOS 18.2's AI advancements:

1. Explore Image Features (Waitlist Access)

- **Genmoji and Image Playground**: These tools allow you to generate personalized emojis and create images from text prompts. While these features are exciting, they're still being gradually rolled out through a waitlist. **Tip**: If you haven't gained immediate access, be patient and offer feedback to Apple to improve the experience 9to5Mac

2. Enhance Siri with ChatGPT Integration

- **Siri's New Powers**: Siri now incorporates GPT-like capabilities, making it more adept at answering complex queries. This means that your assistant can handle nuanced conversations and provide better responses for a wider range of requests. **Tip**: Try asking more detailed, open-ended questions to see how Siri's AI handles them

[The Mac Observer](#)

.

3. Utilize AI for Smart Home Integration

- **HomeKit Automation**: Leverage AI to create smarter home automation routines. iOS 18.2 makes your devices more intuitive, offering personalized suggestions for energy-saving settings and routine adjustments. **Tip**: Set up automation based on your daily habits for seamless home control
  [The Mac Observer](#)

  .

4. Tap into Apple Intelligence for Productivity

- **Smart Recommendations**: Apple's AI can suggest actions based on context, such as recommending apps or reminders based on time, location, or even interactions. **Tip**: Pay attention to these proactive suggestions to streamline your workflow
  [9to5Mac](#)

  .

5. Battery Management with AI

- **Optimize Battery Usage**: AI in iOS 18.2 adjusts power consumption based on the tasks you're performing. If you're using high-demand features like image processing or real-time translation, be mindful of battery drain. **Tip**: Enable **Low Power Mode** when using intensive features for extended periods
  [The Mac Observer](#)

6. AI Privacy Features

- **On-Device Processing**: Apple continues to focus on privacy by processing most AI tasks directly on the device. This minimizes the risk of data misuse. **Tip**: Turn off features you don't use regularly, like background app refresh or constant location tracking, to further secure your privacy
  [AppleInsider](#)

7. Use AI in Content Creation

- **Generate and Edit Content**: From creating text to generating visuals with AI, iOS 18.2 offers powerful tools for artists, creators, and marketers. The Image Playground feature allows for creative exploration through AI-driven tools. **Tip**: Experiment with combining text-based AI generation and image tools to create unique

multimedia content
[The Mac Observer](#)

By understanding these features and utilizing them effectively, you can fully tap into the AI-powered improvements in iOS 18.2. Make sure to engage with Apple's gradual rollouts and take advantage of all the customization options to enhance your daily experience

Printed in Dunstable, United Kingdom